W9-CNE-774

This Book
presented to the

CHURCH
LIBRARY
IN HONOR OF

ROBERT SHELTON

BY

ADULT 3 LADIES CLASS

KINGDOM SEEKERS

Code 4386-22 No. 2, Broadman Supplies, Nashville, Tenn. Printed in USA

Safer Than a Known Way

PAMELA ROSEWELL MOORE

Safer Than a Known Way

BIRDVILLE
BAPTIST CHURCH
LIBRARY

Published by

chosen books

FLEMING H. REVELL COMPANY
OLD TAPPAN, NEW JERSEY

Out of respect for their privacy, the names of some people have been changed.

Unless otherwise noted, Scripture quotations are taken from The Holy Bible, New International Version © 1978 by the International Bible Society, used by permission of Zondervan Bible Publishers.

ISBN 0-8007-9137-1

All rights reserved. No part of this publication may be reproduced, stored in a retrieval system, or transmitted in any form or by any means without the prior permission of the publisher.

A Chosen Book
Copyright © 1988 by Pamela Rosewell Moore

Chosen Books are published by
Fleming H. Revell Company
Old Tappan, New Jersey
Printed in the United States of America

For Sylvia

There have been many who helped me on my journey and they are largely unnamed in this book.

To them and to John and Elizabeth Sherrill, Jane Campbell and Ann McMath who gave encouragement and editorial assistance I want to extend my deep gratitude.

Contents

Contents

Foreword

How do you evaluate God's guidance in your personal life if there is no direct scriptural precedent describing and dealing with exactly *your* situation?

Think about this question: Do we always have to be able to point to just one single Bible verse in order to justify our actions, or more likely to justify our lack of actions? Do we really need a verse from Scripture to paste over our actions like Christian wallpaper? I heard of a dentist who had Psalm 81:10 written out in large letters on the wall opposite the dental chair so that anxious patients could receive inspiration by reading: "Open wide your mouth and I will fill it." That's one way to appropriate a Bible verse!

But, again, do we *have* to?

I am not a very observant person. Pam has probably observed me a lot more than I have her, but she had more reasons for that too. My wife, Corry, once asked Pam the secret of the fabulous sense of loyalty she demonstrated throughout the years she was with me as my personal secretary—not to mention her roles as babysitter and whatever else came her way as part of a small, busy, and terribly overextended team. (Incidentally, my family was overextended too, but for that story you should read *God's Smuggler*.) To this she answered something like: "When

11

Andrew asks me to do something I don't think about it. I first do it and then indulge in the privilege of doubting the wisdom of it later. But it usually proves that Andrew was right. Being a visionary he simply sees more and further than I do.''

What a beautiful attitude!

Now, although I don't regard myself as particularly observant, I do see one very important principle unfolding in Pam's life. She has always been where God could use her to supplement the life or ministry of someone who needed—you guessed it—who needed *Pam*. With all the talents, love, and dedication God has given her, Pam was there to assist in her unique way a person hurt by success, or hurt by a stroke, or hurt by personal calamities—and always her gifts came at the right time, thus enriching many lives.

I know that the word *surrender* is not a very popular one, but the world would be nowhere today if there were not enough people who are willing first of all to do what God asks of them, and secondly to do what people ask of them. There are far too many independent people in the world (and independent people may soon become dispensable people). But those who do what is being asked of them or who simply are in the places where God can use them to fill a void or stand in the gap, make up with their talents what is lacking in a person or ministry. Those persons are definitely indispensable.

I will stop now and you can start reading this fascinating book for yourself. Apart from understanding Pam and me better, it will definitely give you more understanding about our beloved Corrie ten Boom, from one who knew her more intimately than anyone else did. Here is Pam's story.

Brother Andrew
Harderwijk, Holland

"I said to the man who stood at the gate of the year: 'Give me a light that I may tread safely into the unknown.' And he replied: 'Go out into the darkness and put your hand into the hand of God. That shall be to you better than light and safer than a known way.' "

M. L. Haskins

Chapter One

Twenty-Two Words

It was a damp Friday lunchtime in March 1965 and my father, sister, and I were seated at the square dining table in our kitchen. Our small, red-brick home stood on its own at the main gates of a large public garden called Alexandra Park, in Hastings, East Sussex, on the south coast of England.

The kitchen was the coziest room in the house and it was here that our family took all our meals. To my right was a coal fire, much-needed that day, on either side of which were two armchairs with red upholstery. Behind me was the dark oak sideboard in which we kept the crockery and cutlery. To my left, framed by gray curtains with a red pattern, were two large windows that gave a view onto a bank filled with apple trees, their branches now bare. The naked trees and gray skies seemed to reflect my mood.

Dad and I had a few more minutes at home before returning to the offices of the Hastings Parks and Gardens Department where we both worked. Mother was on duty as a ward sister at the Royal East Sussex Hospital and my young brother, Derek, always known as Digger, was having his lunch at Hastings Grammar School where he was a pupil.

My sister, Sylvia, had prepared a meal for the three of us who were home. Steam was rising from beneath the flaky crust of the steak and kidney pie on the plate before me. It was one of my favorite meals, but today it did not look inviting. What on earth had made me agree to go to our church's youth group weekend retreat, due to start this evening? Why had I let my sister talk me into it?

Well, actually, I knew why. There was an unwelcome barrier between Sylvia and me, and at times I found myself agreeing to her suggestions, like going on a youth group weekend, just to please her. Sylvia was two-and-a-half years younger than my twenty-one years. She was at Hastings High School, preparing to enter the University of Sussex later that year. In looks she did not resemble me particularly. I was taller, with very pale skin, dark brown hair, and wide-set brown eyes. Sylvia had mid-brown hair, large gray eyes, and softer features. She did not resemble me in things academic, either (my own school record was far less impressive). She had a great sense of fun and I wished we could be better friends but there was a wall between us. Sylvia was a committed Christian and I was a half-hearted one.

Knowing that her university studies would take her away from home before long and that the coming years might not give many opportunities to be together, I had agreed to attend with her the retreat organized by the youth group of St. Leonards Parish Church, the family home church. The Christian fervor of many of the young people made me extremely uncomfortable.

"Well," said Sylvia, finishing her lunch with enthusiasm and pushing her plate to one side, "you both have to return to work soon and we need to make plans. Will you take Pam and me to the church this evening, Dad? There is a bus leaving there at six-thirty to take us to Ashburnham Place."

"Honey," replied Dad, using his pet name for her, although such an Americanism was unusual in England, "I wish I could but I need the car tonight for a meeting. Isn't there anybody else who could take you?"

"No," I chimed in before Sylvia could reply. We had no friends leaving from this part of town. Since it was Friday, the office would not close until late and I could not get to the church by 6:30 P.M. "I guess we won't be able to go. Let's cancel our places." I felt very relieved at the prospect.

"Oh, we can't do that," said my persistent sister. "I'll order a taxi."

"You make the arrangements then," I told her, with a lack of enthusiasm, placing my knife and fork next to my half-finished lunch.

The hands of the clock were pointing to twenty to two. I had to return to work and there was no time to argue. It looked as if I was going to spend two uncomfortable days at a retreat. Perhaps, though, my going with her would appease Sylvia, whose attitude often needled me. She was always very direct. "Pam," she had said on several occasions, "you say you are a Christian, but are you really trusting the Lord Jesus with all your life?" "Mind your own business," was my reply, but I often felt a pang of conscience for responding in such a way. A few minutes later Dad drove to our office in Alexandra Park and I resumed the day's work. I tried to boost my spirits by telling myself that the retreat would soon be over and I would at least have had the satisfaction of being with her for a few more hours before she left home for the university.

But I was aware that it was not just to please Sylvia that I had said I would go. A power outside my will or Sylvia's had challenged me to join the outing. Having my will challenged annoyed me, but it was a familiar experience. Sylvia, Digger, and I had grown up in a very happy and simple home where a spirit of helpfulness was more important than material possessions. Dad and Mother gave us a strong example of our responsibility toward others in the community. For as long as I could remember, Mother spent nearly every day of the week at the Royal East Sussex Hospital where she was a very good and dearly loved nurse, working long hours of unpaid overtime to help meet the nursing shortage. Small and plump, she had a beautiful, sunny personality and a voice that, even in normal speech, sounded like a song, betraying her Welsh origin. In the evenings and on weekends when Mother was on duty, Dad cooked, cleaned, shopped, ironed, and took care of the three of us children. A very orderly man, he always managed to find time for reading and constantly challenged us to be curious. He knew something about almost any subject that came up. The whole family shared a love of books and words. Our parents had always underlined academic achievement, encouraging us to read a lot and to gain a large vocabulary. Mother and Dad were deeply happy together and Sylvia, Digger, and I grew up having never heard a parental quarrel.

Why, then, I asked myself, did I have an attitude of deep discontent? While I was growing up it could not be said that England as a nation was particularly depressed. There was an optimistic, hopeful feeling in our country in the postwar years. Large-scale rebuilding of the sites bombed during the war of the previous decade took place in the 1950s. The slogan heard very often was: "We have never had it so good," and the whole of Britain looked forward to a bright future.

A few hundred yards from our childhood home was the Anglican parish church of St. Leonards, which we attended regularly. St. Leonards had a nautical theme. The scalloped lines of the masonry suggested waves on the nearby English Channel, and the pulpit, fashioned by a craftsman on the actual shores of Lake Galilee, looked like the prow of a ship. The original church was destroyed in an air raid during the war and our minister, Canon C. C. Griffiths, worked hard to raise money to rebuild it. That was a long task, for in postwar years despite the belief in a bright future, actual cash funds were in short supply. Once, a parishioner expressed concern that there would never be enough money to rebuild the church. "Oh, that is no problem," Canon Griffiths said, "I have a rich father who will provide the money." Then, as the parishioner looked relieved, he pointed upward to heaven and added, "But you have to get to know Him first."

I felt uncomfortable when I heard that story. Could God actually supply needed money? Such faith required trust and I just didn't have that quality. I didn't really trust Him in that way. What if God wanted for me something other than I myself wanted? My feelings were opposite to those expressed in a hymn often sung in our church. One verse frequently returned to my mind uninvited:

> *Praise to the Lord who o'er all things so wondrously*
>   *reigneth,*
> *Shelters thee under his wings, yea, so gently sustaineth!*
> *Hast thou not seen how thy desires e'er have been granted*
>   *in what he ordaineth?*

The hymn claimed that the greatest happiness lay in the discovery and the following of God's will. I did not see how that could be. I wanted to choose my own way and would take it, often, at the expense of my younger brother and sister. An example of this took place at the coronation of Queen Elizabeth II when I was nine years old. There was an air of much excitement before the big day. We children were in for a double treat. Television sets were rare, but we had a great-aunt and uncle who had bought one, and our family was invited to watch the coronation being relayed from Westminster Abbey.

Sylvia, Digger, and I attended the same school a few miles' bus ride along the seafront. Dressed in our green-and-white school uniforms we made the journey together. On the day before the coronation I was called out of class and asked to go to the first-aid room. Sylvia, age seven, had bumped her head and needed to go home. My first thought was not so much of Sylvia as of myself. I hoped whatever accident had befallen my sister would not prevent my viewing the coronation the next day. I made my way to the first-aid room and found Sylvia, not badly hurt but quiet and white-faced, a bandage covering a cut on her head. In her left hand she was holding three wrapped candies. As we walked to the bus stop, I asked Sylvia about the candies. "The teacher gave them to me because I was so good and didn't cry when I hurt my head," she told me. "Hand them over to me," I said, somehow persuading myself that since I had been called out of class I had earned a right to the sweets. Sylvia complied obediently. She was, after all, used to this kind of logic in her older sister.

I ate all of the candy long before we reached home, but I knew that my invention of "rights" was nonsense. As always when I made such claims, I was miserable. The next day, on a small black-and-white television screen, we watched the coronation of Queen Elizabeth II and at first

I believed Sylvia's mishap had disappeared from my mind. Through the years, though, to my annoyance, the crowning of the Queen had been associated not with joy but with the incident of claiming rights that were never mine in the first place.

And now, twelve years later, as I went through the afternoon's work at the office, I hoped that the coming weekend retreat would not contain too many pleas to make a public stand for Jesus Christ. All through my childhood I had been taught that this was the most important thing in life and I had successfully resisted it. Canon Griffiths let no opportunity pass to remind us that it was God's purpose to have a personal relationship with each of His children. "It is not enough to know *about* Jesus," he said. "You have to know Him. You must accept that His death on the cross and His resurrection are the only way to forgiveness and to eternal life."

I believed in Jesus Christ, but Canon Griffiths also stressed that Jesus had to be Lord of all my life, and that I did not like to hear. I wanted to follow Christ from a distance. To follow closely might mean He would ask of me something I could never do. There was a strong emphasis in our church on foreign service. I had observed that real Christians often became missionaries. One elderly Sunday school teacher had been heard to pronounce, "I claim the Rosewell girls for the mission field." I resisted it strongly. I did not want to be "claimed for the mission field." I knew I could not fulfill such a role.

Missionaries spoke at our church frequently. They often spent years in foreign lands, miles away from England. What if God wanted that of me—to live far from my family? No, I could not do that. England was my home, that's where my family was. I was much too timid to think of venturing overseas.

And missionaries were public speakers. I was most definitely not a speaker. Class participation at school had been something I dreaded. When the teacher asked a question I would hold back even when I knew the answer. On the rare occasions when I did venture an answer, my heart beat so hard I knew the rest of the class could hear it. And inevitably the teacher would say, "Speak up, Pamela, nobody can hear you."

But there was yet a third factor, which was by far the most weighty in my being unwilling to commit my life to Jesus Christ. Above everything else, from the time when I was a young child, I wanted a husband and children. What would my husband be like? English, of course, and tall and dark. And our children? We would probably have three, the same number as in our own happy family. No, missionary life was not for me.

The rest of that Friday afternoon in the office passed quickly enough. I left a little before 6 P.M. to be home in time for the taxi that Sylvia had ordered. It did not arrive, but that did not concern Sylvia at first. It was hard to find our little house, tucked away behind the main gates of Alexandra Park. Probably the driver had lost his way. When 6:20 P.M. came, my sister called the taxi company and learned that a mistake had been made and no taxi had been sent.

I breathed a sigh of relief. It was now far too late to reach the church by 6:30 P.M. when the bus left. The matter was settled. We could not go. My sister, however, did not give up. She telephoned the church to explain what had happened and learned that unexpectedly a private car was leaving the church at 8:30 P.M.

As Sylvia's hopes rose, mine sank. Sylvia again ordered a taxi and a short while later, depressed and irritable, I dragged a small overnight case to our front door.

The taxi carried us beneath the ruins of England's earliest Norman castle, built by William the Conqueror after his defeat of King Harold in 1066. I had always felt sorry for Harold, who, with his battle-weary men, had marched here to Hastings from Yorkshire in the north of England. Tired out, Harold met his match in William's fresh troops from Normandy.

The taxi then turned westward along the coast on the road that parallels the English Channel. I had walked along its bordering promenade many times as a teenager, watching the sea. The Channel was often gray, whipped by the prevailing southwesterly wind, throwing frothy breakers against the smooth brown and white pebbles that formed the main part of the beach. How many times had the tide turned since William the Conqueror began to build his castle in 1066? How many people through the last nine centuries had watched these relentless waters come and go, had felt the salt spray on their faces, had breathed this damp and invigorating air? Had they also wondered why they lived? If life had meaning and purpose?

I remembered how, during a walk on the promenade on a damp winter's day, a seagull screeched high above me. I watched as it swooped and ascended, beating its wings strongly against the wind. Suddenly it stopped fighting and gave itself to the wind, allowing its sleek body to be borne along. On that day, long ago, I felt a nudge inside, as if God were asking me to give myself to Him as the bird gave itself to the wind. It did not fall but was carried strongly as its own efforts ceased. Why was I remembering that *now?* I was careful not to tell Sylvia who would certainly have made some irritating point that I did not want to hear.

We arrived too early and made our way into a cafe

where we ordered coffee. I rummaged in my handbag for my cigarettes and lit one slowly. I knew that would annoy Sylvia, who always had an infuriating way of letting me know it. She never told me she disliked it. She told me God disliked it. Sure enough, she did not let this opportunity go by.

"You should not do that," she said, her gray eyes looking steady and serious. "Smoking is bad for you. It is wrong to harm your body. God tells us in the Bible that we are not our own property, but were bought with a high price when the Lord Jesus gave His life for us."

At that point our coffee arrived. "Don't you tell me what to do," I hurled at Sylvia as soon as the waitress had left the table. "This is my life and I will do what I want with it."

I was fuming. Sylvia did not try to argue with me and there would have been no point, for I had retreated into silence. After finishing our coffee we walked along the seafront to the church where after a few minutes our ride appeared. We climbed aboard and while I remained sullen, Sylvia chatted to the driver who headed into the Sussex countryside.

At last the car pulled through some large gates onto a long driveway that led to Ashburnham Place near the town of Battle, appropriately named, from the mood I was in. It was dark. The narrow road was lit only by the headlights of the car. Shadows from tall trees loomed across the winding road and when the headlights caught smaller trees and bushes as the car swung around curves, they turned them into whimsical shapes that seemed to echo the sense of unreality that I was feeling. *What* was I doing here?

Gradually, as we traveled the narrow road, I became aware of something. There was peace in this place, even in the darkness. I could almost touch it. I realized that it had penetrated my sullenness. The car passed on to a broader, more open road and I could dimly make out a lake to the right, surrounded by trees. The driver pulled up near a large building. We got out, retrieved our small suitcases, and entered a reception area where our presence was registered by a hostess. I continued to sense a deep peace in this place.

The hostess told us that if we hurried we could attend the evening's last meeting, which was just starting in the library. She ushered us into a large room where the group of young people from St. Leonards was seated. In front of them stood a speaker. Ken Habershon was his name, the hostess whispered, and he worked with a Christian mission in London. I had never heard of him.

Sylvia and I found a place toward the back of the room and Mr. Habershon started his talk. I do not recall what he spoke about because my shield of resistance had been raised.

But suddenly, well into his address, one sentence startled me awake. Twenty-two words, but they were spotlighted as if by God Himself and I knew they were meant just for me. It was as if there were nobody else in the universe, except me and God. They were very simple words, but after they were spoken, a new battle began. Not between me and my sister, or between me and an evangelist, but between me and God.

"When Jesus Christ died for you," the speaker said, "it was as if all the dustbins in the world were being emptied on His head."

The words hit me with tremendous force. What a description of my selfishness, my bad temper, and endless discontent. My sin would fill every trashcan in the world, and it had been dumped on the head of Jesus. I remembered the Scripture Sylvia had quoted earlier this evening, "You are not your own, you have been bought with a price." Never before had I understood how humiliating the ransom price had been. I was aware of a great sense of urgency in my heart now. From this moment on it had to be all or nothing. I either followed Jesus Christ whole-heartedly or I did not follow Him at all.

Yet I still hesitated, for instinctively I understood that there was a price I had to pay too. Jesus let my sins—the rotten, stinking sins we all carry, plus my own particular ones—pour over Him; in response I had to surrender to Him all my own "rights." I do not remember the end of the meeting or the refreshments or the conversations that followed, only that a fierce tug-of-war was taking place between my will and God's will. I must have said good-night to my sister, who shared a room with friends in another part of the building, but I do not remember doing so. I do know that when I got into bed in the linoleum-floored dormitory called the "White Room," which I shared with three other girls, I lay and stared into the night, struggling with God, long after everyone else was asleep.

Moonlight through long windows dimly lit our high-ceilinged room. I slipped out of the covers and knelt on a throw rug that covered the cold linoleum.

This was a momentous night. I was sure of it. God, whom I had resisted for so long, had suddenly revealed Himself to me. What would the future hold if I really trusted Jesus, if I surrendered to Him all my past, present, and future? With no conditions? With no "rights" with-held, belonging to me? If I was no longer my own, I had no rights. Not to my own will. Not to my own self.

In the darkness, on my knees, I weighed the matter. What would be the worst that could happen, I asked myself? It could be that God would ask me to do some of the things I feared—three in particular that I had rebelled against almost since my childhood: leaving my family and country, speaking in public, being single.

As I struggled I became aware very strongly of God's presence. I could feel His love for me so deeply that it was almost tangible. His will seemed irresistible. The house was still. The deep, even breathing of my companions told me that they were sound asleep. Then the words of the hymn that, since childhood, often came into my mind uninvited now returned, this time with comfort:

Praise to the Lord, who o'er all things so wondrously
   reigneth,
Shelters thee under his wings, yea, so gently sustaineth!
Hast thou not seen how thy desires e'er have been granted
   in what he ordaineth?

A conviction came over me that I should make way for the will of God. As far as I was able, I then made an unconditional surrender of my will to God. My prayer went something like this:

"Father, thank You for revealing the depth of Your love for me and for not leaving me even though I have resisted You for so long. I now give up my right to my own will. I want to do Your will and be used by You. I will trust You with whatever the future holds. If You want me to work in a foreign country, I will. If You want me to speak in public, although it seems quite impossible, I will. And if You want me to be single in Your service, I will be. I will never seek a marriage partner. If You want me to marry, I will trust You to bring somebody to me. I give You all rights to myself. Amen."

At that moment of relinquishment to God, He gave me

a very beautiful and unusual gift. It came straight from heaven and earthly words fail to convey its reality.

Time seemed to stand still. The discouragement, self-seeking, and introversion, which had always been my companions, gave way to a joy so satisfying that for the first time I felt I was fulfilling the purpose for which I was made. "So, Lord," I said, "this is what being in Your presence means." I remembered that the Bible says, "In Your presence is fullness of joy." And then came a peace and tranquillity by which I knew beyond all doubt that my future was perfectly safe with Him.

But the strongest confirmation of the presence of God was His love. It was as if I were in a sea full of love. Wave upon wave of love broke over my head, strong and irresistible. It had a holy quality and grew so intense that I had to pray, "Lord God, please stop it. Please save some of this for heaven."

After some time I got back into bed but before I fell into the most peaceful sleep of my life I reviewed the incredible evening. The surrender had not taken long, but I knew that it was real and that it would last. What was different about this from what I had expected? Then I thought I knew. I had always assumed that the relinquishing of my will would mean a mighty effort on my part. But the struggle had not lasted for a long time. Even the surrender had been His. God had revealed His love to me and had moved into my life on this particular night, giving me grace to surrender.

When the sun rose over Ashburnham Place the next morning, it was onto a different world. I took a walk early in the morning and saw the house and grounds in the light for the first time. The house was two stories high in the center with a one-story wing on each side. It was of red brick with cream paintwork on its many windows. I discovered that the beautifully landscaped, tree-filled grounds contained three lakes. But it was not just the different surroundings that made everything seem new. It was as if the world were a different place. The grass was a deeper green than I had ever seen, the air was fresher, the sun brighter. I explored the grounds with delight, looking forward to the time when I could share my amazing secret.

Making my way back to the house a little before eight, I went to the dining room just as a group, including Sylvia, was entering for breakfast. I was less curious about the breakfast, which promised to be delicious, judging by the aroma, than I was about the group's reaction. I wondered if they, and especially my sister, would notice anything different. Surely they would.

Tables were set with white chinaware and I seated myself at one of them with Sylvia and a few others. I noticed that she was observing me closely, but she said nothing. When all the tables had been filled and grace had been said, we began to help ourselves to cereal, eggs and bacon, coffee and tea.

Richard, who was the group clown, regarded me with interest. "Pam," he said, "you look very happy today. What has happened this early in the morning?"

Suddenly, although there was a lot of talking and laughing taking place in the room, all was quiet. Everyone was looking my way. I was particularly aware of my sister.

Shyness and a determination to answer the question struggled inside me for a while, and then determination won.

"When I came to Ashburnham last night, I was set in my mind that nobody was going to persuade me to become a committed Christian," I told them. "But something happened at last night's meeting. I have given my life to God in a new way, nothing held back."

The group around the table expressed their happiness at this surprising news, but there was no deeper joy than that which I read in Sylvia's eyes. I was sure that she had seen the change in me as soon as we met that morning. I was aware of a new and deep relationship between us. This time yesterday I had wished that she and I could become better friends. We were now not only friends, but sisters in the truest sense of the word. I looked forward to the opportunity to show her that this change was real. How surprised we both would have been if we had known how and where God's will was to lead me in the coming years. There were changes ahead that I could never have imagined.

Chapter Two

A Good Way to Begin

When I returned home next morning, my new peace went with me, but hovering in the back of my mind was a question. It had to do with Bob Tanner.

Red-haired, serious, and five years older than I, Bob was a draughtsman at a firm in Southampton, a large southern English port one hundred miles to the west. We had met when a schoolfriend and I took a vacation in Spain the previous autumn. Bob's visits and letters had become more and more frequent, and I knew he was becoming fond of me. I liked him and before this last weekend thought that our relationship might ripen into love. I sensed that a marriage proposal was imminent.

But what about my prayer of relinquishment in the linoleum-floored dormitory room at Ashburnham Place? I had "given my whole life to God" but what did that mean, really? The moonlit commitment now had to be worked out in the bright light of today.

The problem was clear to me. Bob did not go to church and although we had not discussed Christianity at any length, I was sure he was not a Christian. Should I give Bob up straightaway, or would I perhaps be able to persuade him to become a Christian? I needed advice and the best person to ask was Sylvia.

That Monday evening after supper I asked Sylvia to come upstairs to the bedroom we shared; she seated herself on her twin bed with its pink bedspread and I sat on mine.

"Sylvia, I want to ask your advice about Bob," I began. "I think he is getting serious, and I don't want to give him up but . . . Bob's not a Christian. Should I keep seeing him? Maybe the Lord will use me to help him become a Christian."

I knew that I could depend on a direct answer from my sister, whether I liked the answer or not. "No," Sylvia said, "it does not work that way. The Bible tells us very clearly that a believer and an unbeliever do not have anything in common and that's no basis for marriage. And the Bible says even more strongly that light and darkness cannot have any fellowship. You can read it in Second Corinthians six. I believe that you must make a complete break with Bob. The Lord will give you the strength to do what is right."

Sylvia went downstairs to do some homework, and I took my Bible and read the passage she had told me about. It really seemed to be clear, but it was so difficult and I found myself thinking in terms of the "rights" I had so blithely surrendered three evenings before, especially at this moment my right to a rich and satisfying relationship with a man. I did not want to give up that hope. If I spoke frankly with Bob it might even drive him away from the Lord!

Getting on my knees on the floral carpet I was honest with God about how I felt. There was deep sorrow in my heart. Tears spilled onto the pink bedspread. I knew that if I were to give up Bob I was not just giving up this one person, but all he represented—an assumption that I would marry.

As I prayed, I saw that it was necessary for me to relinquish all hold on this previously held right to determine my own life. I had to do what God told me to do and trust Him entirely. Bob was God's responsibility, not mine. Then, suddenly, I knew for myself that I had to put my faith in action by ending this friendship. God would take care of the consequences in Bob's life. If he was going to become a Christian, God did not need me to show him the way. I relinquished Bob to God very definitely, and then, through my tears, it happened again. I was immersed in a sea of love as I had been that evening in the dormitory. Billows of love were flowing over me and again I had to ask the Lord to stop their intensity. I knew that I had made the right decision.

I got up, went immediately to my dressing table, and took out my pen and writing paper. Through a mixture of tears and joy I wrote to Bob Tanner and explained what had happened to me at Ashburnham Place and why I had to end our friendship. I told him that above everything else I wanted him to come to know the Lord Jesus too. Then I waited. A few days later a bewildered letter came in reply, indicating that he did not understand. I thought it best not to answer his letter and did not hear from Bob again. During the next few weeks as my joy continued, I was grateful that I had learned an important principle in surrendering my will to God, which is to *obey quickly.*

I did want my newfound joy, and the reason for it, to be obvious to others. Mother and Dad were private people when it came to talking about personal faith and I decided not to say anything to them about my new life. I wanted them to see it for themselves. It was not long before a remark of Dad's made it clear that they had indeed noticed. "You have been different since that weekend at Ashburnham," he said. "Much happier."

Other changes began to take place, too, during the spring of 1965. I found myself busier than ever before. I participated in all the activities of our youth group and attended as many church functions as possible. I was asked to undertake the task of secretary to the young people's fellowship, and then to teach a Sunday school class of very small children. Although I had very little teaching experience I could not resist the challenge. I was beginning to learn to reverse the shy and defeatist attitude that had been with me from childhood. "I can do all things through Christ who strengthens me," I read in the Bible. I thought it would be a way to learn to grow in faith if I allowed myself to be put into positions where I had to prove the truth of that verse. And what better way was there, I decided, than to make myself very busy in the Lord's service?

Where was I, then? I had made a general surrender of my rights, including that of my own will, to the Lord, and He had given me a confirming peace. I had made one difficult surrender of a specific "right"—to my relationship with Bob. Energy and freedom followed. Now what was He going to do? How would He show me my next step?

If there was one person apart from my sister whom God used to help me in my Christian life it was our tall, handsome curate, Clive Boddington. He and his wife, Daphne, proved to be an enormous strength to me during the first year of fuller Christian life. Their home—although small and crowded with baby things—was always open to me and any of the members of our group. Once his curacy in St. Leonards was over, Clive hoped to be a missionary in Kenya, East Africa. He talked about his dreams, directing the vision of our group far beyond the confines of our borders. He often brought to our attention the needs of a great deal of the world that had not heard the Gospel and taught us to pray about those needs.

As Clive taught us to intercede I began to realize that God often makes the person who prays part of the answer to the prayer. In my times of prayer the thought began to come to me that I should apply to do some service abroad. How was it possible that a thought previously alien to all I desired could seem so natural now? Part of me felt incredulous even discussing it with Clive. Leave my home? Yet when Clive encouraged me to go, I wanted to.

The reaction at home, however, was less hearty. "Your father and I really want you to do whatever makes you happy," said Mother, "but I don't know how well you would do so far away from home." She reminded me that I was a home-loving person and that a previous effort to leave home had not worked out well.

She was referring to something that had happened four years before, when I was eighteen. At the time of my graduation from high school I had not thought much about a career. My aim was to marry young but I also knew that I needed to go to work while waiting for the right person. Unlike the United States, England does not have college education available to anybody who wants it. University places in England are given only to those with serious academic aspirations and those I did not have.

All my life I had greatly admired my mother and had seen how fulfilling nursing was to her. I applied for Nurses' Training School in the town of Canterbury, about fifty miles northeast of Hastings. At first the work was theoretical. I enjoyed that part. Anatomy and physiology fascinated my analytical mind. Then came the practice and that was another matter altogether. I found I could not cope with nursing serious illnesses. It depressed me to deal with patients who would soon die. Being far from home—fifty miles away!—I was isolated and insecure. I wanted desperately to quit but could not face the indignity of failure.

If the curtain that divides time from eternity had been moved aside for a minute, I would have seen how God was to take this apparent failure and the preliminary nursing experience I gained at bedsides in Canterbury, England, and use them at another bedside, many years later, during the final significant illness of an old Dutch woman who, many agree, was one of God's greatest gifts to His Church in our century. But I did not know it then.

How was I to escape from a career in which I absolutely did not fit? The matter was decided for me. After a heavy cold, a cough persisted and so did a high temperature. Lobar pneumonia was diagnosed, which necessitated a two-week stay in a hospital and several weeks of convalescence. In view of the fact that I would now have lost so many weeks' study, I decided that this would be a good time to make a graceful exit from Nurses' Training School and tendered my resignation.

So . . . I returned home. Where, I thought to myself, I belonged. One day during my weeks of convalescence, Dad showed me an advertisement for a clerk/shorthand typist in his department of the local authority. I applied, was accepted, and had, now in late 1965, worked there for almost four years. My mother was right. I was a home-loving person and knew little about living even in a town fifty miles away much less in foreign countries.

But the Lord was beginning to show me how He could set me free if I didn't hold my rights closely. He had given me courage to serve in the church and Sunday school during this past year, a work I once would have been too unsure of myself to handle. Was more ahead? One evening, alone in the upstairs bedroom, I was reading Ephesians chapter two. The tenth verse struck me with remarkable force: "We are [God's] workmanship, created in Christ Jesus unto good works, which God hath before ordained that we should walk in them" (KJV).

That verse seemed to be telling me that God had my way all planned if only I would get out of my own way with my own plans. There were works prepared for me to do. All I had to do was find them. What a wondrous promise! It took the strain of life away. It meant that I did not have to struggle up any career ladder. All I needed to know was how to find the works God had prepared for me to do. I began to ask Him in prayer what those works were and now—incredibly—I believed He was leading me to apply for work abroad.

Half hoping that I would not be needed, I wrote to the Church Missionary Society in London, the Anglican Church's missionary organization. I explained that I had had nearly four years' secretarial experience and wondered if there was a short-term service for which they might consider me. I was careful to emphasize "short-term." If I was not cut out for it I could surely bear it for a limited time.

A lot sooner than I expected, a letter came back from the London headquarters. They had been very glad to hear from me because they wanted to fill a need in the country of Kenya, East Africa. What a coincidence! Kenya was the country to which our curate, Clive Boddington, and his family hoped to be moving. Even if I only saw them rarely it was a comfort to know a family from home would be in Kenya too. The Archbishop of East Africa's secretary was overworked and the office was in need of help. If my interview with headquarters and my references proved satisfactory I could leave for the capital city, Nairobi, in which the Archbishop's headquarters were situated, as soon as arrangements could be made. It would be necessary for me to have the money for my air ticket in advance, but I would receive housing and a small salary in Nairobi. The appointment would be for one year with the possibility of staying longer if mutually agreeable.

I did not know it then, but I was seeing a pattern I would recognize many times in the future. The pattern was this: first *surrender*, then *wait*, then *walk*. First surrender your own will and plans; then wait until you are convinced you've heard God's direction; then walk in the work He has planned beforehand for you to walk in.

Before beginning to "walk" too far I wanted to be as certain as I could that I was heading in the right direction. It was not enough to "hear from the Lord" and run off to Africa. What if it had been a hunch of my own? I needed to submit the idea to our minister, Clive Boddington, and receive his go-ahead and the blessing of the church. I also asked several friends whom I knew had close fellowship with the Lord if they would pray for me.

During the time of waiting for the approval of my references, for the interview in London, and for the necessary medical examination, I certainly had some times of anxiety. I could not really imagine taking a plane by myself and flying to Africa, but I tried not to rely on my imagination. I made myself take hold of the verse that had stood out for me so strongly. "We are [God's] workmanship, created in Christ Jesus unto good works, which God hath before ordained that we should walk in them."

As I proceeded with the plans I found that my heart was at peace. And I knew that the peace was a mark of God's approval. So was the blessing of the church leadership. If those elements had not been there, I believe I would have known it was not right to go ahead with those particular plans.

The weeks went by quickly. My references were approved, the interview in London was positive, the medical examination was passed, and plans could now be made for departure. In August 1966 I tendered my resignation at my place of work, arranging for the end of September to be my leaving date.

The next hurdle was paying for the ticket. My family was very supportive and would have helped me had I wanted them to, but I preferred to be self-supporting, which actually was good because it allowed me to watch other ways God has of supplying His people's needs. The cost of a ticket to Nairobi was about £150. I had £120 in my savings account and therefore needed thirty more before the projected departure date of October 20, 1966. How would I get it? It seemed such a large amount, the equivalent of several weeks of work at the job I had just left.

It happened that earlier I had studied for and taken an examination, the passing of which would result in a raise in salary at the office. One day the mail brought the good news of a successful result and I was given a salary increment that, with back pay, amounted to about twenty pounds. Ten more were needed. These arrived in the form of two gifts of five pounds each from members of our church. It was the first time I had ever received gifts like that. One of the givers—a very quiet, middle-aged single woman—I hardly knew. How could she have known of my need? Into my memory came the story about Canon Griffiths' "rich father" who would supply all that was needed. "But you have to get to know Him first," Canon Griffiths had said, pointing upward. I had found it hard to believe that God would give guidance in such practical ways, even to the provision of money. Now I was seeing it for myself.

As the summer of 1966 passed into autumn, I felt my excitement mounting. What would it be like to live outside England? What kinds of adventures were awaiting me? But I also had to admit to some deep apprehensions. Africa was so very far away. The old fear of leaving my home country for as long as a year began to rise in me.

One day I heard a story that encouraged me. A young African minister was in England for seminary study and had the opportunity to preach to a rather sleepy and staid congregation who must have been surprised at his opening words: "No go, no lo. No go, no lo." Before they could reach the conclusion that he was speaking to them in his own African language, the young man quoted Matthew 28: "Go ye therefore, and teach all nations . . . and, lo, I am with you always, even unto the end of the world" (KJV). The young African explained that the "lo" of "I am with you always" depends on the "go" of "into all the world." If we are not fulfilling the Lord's will for us, there is no promise that we will know His presence with us.

I laughed at the story, but I kept thinking of the four words. I took them as an encouragement to remember that whatever happened, the Lord would be with me, and repeated "No go, no lo" when fear threatened my peace.

As it happened, though, I was not to leave for Kenya without knowing that once in the country I would almost certainly meet up not only with our curate Clive Boddington and his family, but also with Colin and Mary, two of the members of our youth group who had been assigned to projects in Pumwani, a slum quarter of Nairobi.

So, I began to assemble items necessary for the journey. Passport, new luggage, medical certificates, books, and, of course, the necessary clothes.

Some encouraging letters had reached me from Elizabeth Swayne, the Archbishop's secretary whom I was to assist. Elizabeth was an American, had worked in Kenya for several years, and was looking forward, she said, to meeting me at Nairobi Airport when my plane arrived on October 21. She described herself as middle-aged, with white hair, and said she would be looking out for me. She sounded very confident, having obviously had years of experience not only of secretarial work, but of living in Africa. I hoped the secretarial experience I had had would be sufficient to help her in her duties. All was set for the journey to begin.

On the evening of October 20, 1966, my parents, brother, sister, a former workmate, and I crowded into Dad's Ford Consul and he drove under a gray and wintry sky to London's Heathrow Airport, a journey of about two-and-a-half hours from our home.

I could hear the droning of the jets overhead as we approached the airport and could smell the fuel of the aircraft. Airports were not familiar to me. This would be just the second time I had flown. The first time had been on a small aircraft two years before when I went on vacation to Spain. This flight was to be on a large intercontinental jet, a VC10 of the British Overseas Airways Corporation.

Dad parked the car, we took my two suitcases from the trunk, and the six of us walked to the check-in counter and then to passport control. Before passing through, I took leave of everybody. As I was about to leave them Sylvia handed me a package. It was a copy of the Phillips New Testament! I had to turn away quickly for fear of breaking into tears right there in the terminal. The customs official checked my papers, then waved me through the barrier and I was alone. Surrounded by hundreds of people, yet alone.

Holding my purse in one hand and my cabin luggage in the other I turned to wave a final goodbye to my family and friend whom I thought would still be visible behind the customs counter. Sure enough they were. I don't know how it happened, but I tripped and landed on my knees amidst all the other passengers. This was mortifying, but as I struggled to stand up I heard someone in my group at the barrier call out: "That is a good way to begin, on your knees." They had never said a truer word. There would need to be much prayer in the year lying ahead.

Chapter Three

Lessons from Loneliness

The plane winged its way into the night leaving England, then Europe, far behind me. With the dawn I could see we were flying over arid, unrelieved beige sand dunes, which looked the same hundreds of miles after hundreds of miles. This was the Sahara Desert and I was amazed by the size of it. After what seemed hours the terrain below began to look more tropical and this scenery continued for several more hours. I was tired but at the same time excited. What would Kenya be like—if we ever got there!

At last we began our descent and I could see that we were going to be landing southeast of the city. I had never seen so much open space. The plane landed and taxied to its gate. I gathered my hand baggage and made my way to the door with the other passengers, curious whether or not it would be easy to recognize Elizabeth Swayne. When I made my way down the steps and across the tarmac a wave of warm air swept over me. England, hours before, had been cold and damp. And there was something else very different. It was the light. Very strong, it pricked my eyes. I groped around in my handbag for my new sunglasses.

A white-haired woman was waiting beyond customs

and I knew immediately that this was Elizabeth Swayne. She seemed to recognize me, too, and we greeted each other enthusiastically.

"Welcome to Kenya," she said, in her foreign American accent. "Let me help you with your bags." Following in Elizabeth's wake, I began to notice the cosmopolitan nature of the crowd around us, with, not surprisingly, more blacks than whites. I hoped I would make black friends in Kenya.

So far so good, I thought, as we piled my bags into Elizabeth's little Volkswagen with its steering wheel on the right. At least that was the same as in England. As she started the car, Elizabeth looked at me thoughtfully as if sizing up how tired I was. "I think we'll drive you home by Nairobi National Park," she said. "It was Kenya's first wildlife reserve."

I gave an enthusiastic yes and as we were driving toward the park through expanses of yellowish grass, Elizabeth gave me some facts about the country. "Kenya is a very new nation," she said. "It was declared a republic less than two years ago. The people of Kenya are, of course, very proud of it. There is a Swahili word you are going to hear often, *harambee*. It means 'pulling together for the common good.' Kenya is a country of many tribes and languages and its people are learning to work together."

As we pulled through the gates of Nairobi National Park, my eyes began to adjust to the bright light and the expanse of straw-colored coarse and high grass. Here and there a low thorn tree afforded some shade. In front of us was a range of beautiful hills whose name, I learned, was the Ngongs. Gradually, as Elizabeth pointed them out to me, I began to notice birds and animals whose colors, at first, seemed to blend with the grass and make them invisible. "If you look over there in the tall grass under the thorn tree you will see a pride of lions lying down. They are taking their afternoon siesta and after sunset will begin hunting. They are sleepy, but we must not take any risks. Keep the windows rolled up."

As I watched the lions in fascination, Elizabeth shifted ground and began to tell me a little about the extent of the territory for which my new boss, Dr. Leonard Beecher, Archbishop of the Church of the Province of East Africa, was responsible. The Province included the countries of Kenya and Tanzania. Elizabeth spoke of the work with the facility that years of experience as his secretary afforded her. She seemed very efficient and I was glad that I would have her leadership and guidance during my upcoming year in Kenya.

Then Elizabeth made me clench my teeth with a piece of news.

"Early this morning," she said, driving slowly through the park, "while you were on your flight from London, I received a telephone call from a very good friend of mine. He is a doctor here in Nairobi. He asked me to be his wife and I accepted his proposal. We will be getting married as soon as arrangements can be made. Isn't it good timing that you have arrived just now?"

I was happy for her and told her so. But I also felt stunned and hoped that my next question would not educe the answer I thought it would.

"Will you be staying on as the Archbishop's secretary?"

"For a short while," she replied, "until you have learned the ropes. I will be leaving after that."

My heart sank. How on earth could I, who knew nothing about this country, people, and culture, take over such a big task as secretary to the Archbishop? As Elizabeth left the game park and headed the car toward Nairobi I was silent. I had thought that during my year here all I would need to do was to follow her directions, but now she was leaving. The thought came to me that the Lord was "throwing me into the deep end." I wondered whether I would be able to swim. And then my apprehension was taken over by a quiet resolve. The Lord had brought me safely to this country. It must be true that nothing could be asked of me that was beyond His strength.

The next hours continued to be filled with sights and sounds thus far outside my experience. Elizabeth drove into the city and the most fascinating of the new sights was the people. I had not known there were so many shades of black. Trying not to stare, I made a surreptitious study of the faces of the citizens of Nairobi. I found them very handsome, with their beautiful skin colors ranging from dark olive to ebony. Swahili and Kikuyu were the main tribal languages, I was told, although many understood English.

Then there was the striking beauty of this modern city of Nairobi itself with its new buildings and skyline. Jacaranda trees lined many of its streets and avenues. Never had I seen blue like that. There was much open space in the city, too, and the earth was red. *Murram* was its Swahili name and the smell of it seemed to give a deep connection with the land. So much of my England was cemented in. Here there were expanses of red earth. The scent of dozens of tropical blossoms mingled and filled the air as we drove through gracious suburbs to the part of the city that was to be my home. All of Nairobi was not like this, though, Elizabeth hastened to explain. On the other side of the city were lean-to shacks and the smell of sweat and refuse filled the air.

My new home was on State House Avenue, which street also contained the official residences of President Jomo

Kenyatta and other high government officials. The residence and offices of Dr. Beecher was called "Bishopsbourne." Built of gray stone, it reminded me of a large English country house. An unpaved road from the highway ended in a circular driveway in front of the house and in the center of the driveway was a large round flower bed filled with palms and tropical plants.

On the same grounds as Bishopsbourne were several buildings of differing sizes that were housing for various missionaries connected with the Anglican Church. Elizabeth Swayne took me to her small, cozy house and led me to the spare bedroom. I delighted in the Hibiscus and banana palms with which the house was surrounded and was somewhat shocked by the bars covering all the windows. I had never seen anything like it before and needed to have it explained to me that this was to prevent burglars from breaking in.

How different everything was here, the sounds of the night, for instance. Since Kenya was on the equator, night came very suddenly and the darkness was soon filled with the chirping of crickets. On that first night, toward the break of day, I was awakened by a scream. Running to Elizabeth's room, I was informed by my sleepy hostess that I was to go back to bed and not worry. It was only the peacock owned by Charles Njonjo, the country's Attorney General who was our neighbor on the opposite side of the street.

In the morning, Elizabeth and I walked the twenty-second stroll on the Bishopsbourne compound between her small house and the Archbishop's residence and office and I was introduced to Dr. Beecher and his wife, Gladys. A tall and handsome man, the Archbishop was white and originally from England but had lived in Kenya for many years and was a naturalized citizen.

Mrs. Beecher had been born in Kenya, a member of the family of the paleontologists, Drs. Louis and Mary Leakey. She wore her graying hair pulled back into a bun and had a kind face. The Beechers were probably in their mid-sixties. They gave me a very warm welcome to their home and work and took me on a short tour of the house. The Archbishop's office was in the main part of the house and the office Elizabeth and I were to share until she left to be married was a converted garage on the right-hand side of the house, rectangular in shape and quite plain. There were two desks and chairs. Dusty boxes of files accounted for one wall and filing cabinets, another. At the front of the office, next to the door, louvered windows gave a view of the circular driveway. *So this is to be my workplace for the next year.*

During the next days and weeks, with lots of encouragement from the Archbishop and from Elizabeth, I learned what my new tasks were to be. Slowly the strange-sounding African names became familiar as I directed correspondence all over East Africa in connection with diocesan affairs, helped with arrangements for local meetings and visitors, answered the telephone, and accomplished the variety of small tasks always associated with administration. There was much to do but I found that when I asked the Lord for help He always gave it. I was beginning to know Him in a new way now that most of the things I had relied on in England were very far away.

Elizabeth Swayne's preparations for her marriage meant that her time at the office became shorter. The day came—all too rapidly—when Elizabeth said goodbye. I was glad for the rounds of farewells and good wishes, for they helped cover up a bit of the panic I was feeling.

Now I was alone in the office. But the Archbishop's instruction and patience, Elizabeth's thorough teaching, and my previous secretarial experience resulted in my being well able, with the Lord's help, to cope with the work. I wondered why I had worried about something that had not come to pass and hoped I would remember in the future that worry is a rather useless activity. But there was something else that was very hard for me to bear. It was the loneliness.

My previous curate, Clive Boddington, and his family were now in Kenya and so were Colin and Mary, the two members of our youth group. I met up with all of them fairly often, but oddly, seeing them sometimes served to heighten, not lighten, my homesickness. I had taken over Elizabeth's small house and was living alone, although surrounded by missionaries on the Bishopsbourne compound. They were very kind and often invited me to eat with them, yet I could not help but feel that I was intruding. After living most of my life with a close supportive family I sometimes felt I just could not bear to be alone. But I did not want anyone to know how I felt but instead hoped everyone would think that I was coping well.

Archbishop and Mrs. Beecher did all they could to make the shy newcomer welcome and I ate lunch with them in their dining room during the working week. There were many times, however, when they had to be away on safari. This Swahili word originally meant "a hunting expedition" in English, but has come to mean taking a journey, venturing out into the bush. Dr. Beecher needed to visit far-flung parts of his province and that meant I was left alone in the little garage-office at Bishopsbourne.

One morning before work, when the Archbishop and his wife were away, I decided that I was going to attack the problem of my loneliness with resolution. During my quiet time at home I took the Phillips New Testament that

Sylvia had given me. In black ink in her firm handwriting on the flyleaf she had written: "To Pam, with lots of love from Sylvia. October 1966. Matthew 28:19–20. No go, no lo." Turning to those verses in the Bible, I read them as if they were a prayer. "Father, it says here that You ask Your followers to go and make disciples of all nations. That is why I came to Kenya. I want my life to be used to help others come to know You. And it also says here that if Your children obey You, You will be with them always. Why, then, do I feel so alone? If You are with me, surely I do not need to be so lonely. Please help me to resolve this. Amen."

Straightening my back with new resolve, I locked the door of my little house and walked along the dirt pathway through a green bower and approached Bishopsbourne and my office. I noticed some mauve lilies blooming in the circular flower bed in front of the residence and I remembered how in England we always had so many flowers. Walking to the office door I let myself in, knowing that I was in for a long day alone. The Archbishop's small African staff would be carrying out their duties in the house and grounds, but they spoke little English and there would not be much contact there.

I began my duties and soon found that I was choosing things that put me in contact with people, even if only on paper. I looked through files from previous years, and this gave me some company as I read about the Kenyans and how their country was changing now that independence had come. After about half-an-hour I replaced the papers in the dusty buff files opposite my desk and resumed typing. The day outside was bright and warm, but it was dark and oppressive in the little office. I opened the louvered windows wider and looked at the lilies for a little while. In the distance I saw the Archbishop's Kikuyu gardener. What was his name? Keilah? I wished he could speak English. How good it would be to have some company, even Keilah's, whose brow was always wrinkled as if in a perpetual frown. Maybe the man needed glasses. Whatever the cause of the scowl his face struck me as rather forbidding. I wondered how my family in England was and wanted to pick up the telephone and call them. But at the same time I knew it was good that I could not afford to do so. It would be too embarrassing for anybody, even the Archbishop's African staff, to know how lonely I was. They would probably just call it what I did—a case of ordinary homesickness.

At lunchtime I had a sandwich and walked around the Bishopsbourne compound for a while, but this did not provide any company as the missionaries were away at their tasks in various parts of the city.

The day dragged by. I remembered my prayer that morning that the Lord help me resolve my loneliness. There certainly had been no answer yet! Toward the end of the afternoon I was so discouraged that I felt tears pricking the back of my eyes. Fighting them, I attacked the draft of the minutes of a recent synod meeting. It was no good. I felt tears rolling down my cheeks.

Suddenly, to my horror, I heard the sound of somebody approaching the office door and through the window I saw Keilah walking toward me carrying a hoe, his face as frown-creased as ever. Of all times for somebody to arrive. I did not want him to see my tears. It would be a humiliation. Keilah was leaning his hoe against the front of the building, opening the door, and soon he stood inside with his green plastic flip-flop sandals, ragged khaki shorts, and dirty short-sleeved shirt. He was, I knew, the last person who could help me.

"*Jambo, memsahib,*" said the gardener, giving me the

usual Swahili greeting. He stopped and peered through the dim indoor light and I knew he could see my tear-stained face.

Then, with just the beginning of a smile, Keilah launched into a Kikuyu passage, but when he saw that I was not understanding he stopped, thought hard, and spoke just two words. "No alone," Keilah said, and as he spoke he pointed upward. Then he indicated that he needed a key from my desk drawer and soon departed with a more friendly smile than I thought he was capable of giving.

"No alone!" As I watched Keilah's departing form, I knew that the Lord had given me my answer at two depths. First was the realization that loneliness and aloneness are different things. My life in Kenya would hold some lonely times, but God had never promised that I would not be lonely, only that I would never be alone. He was always with me no matter how I felt and He would often use unexpected voices, like Keilah's, to say so. The second depth of God's answer had to do with never wanting to appear weak. He had arranged for a Kikuyu gardener, with whom I could not converse, to teach me both levels of truth. My reluctance to let anybody know about my loneliness had really been pride. God had arranged for the gardener to arrive at my deepest point of need. Seeing my "weakness" he responded.

Back in my little house that evening I made another prayer of surrender—of my right to be strong. "Father, this morning I asked You to help me to deal with loneliness. I was so afraid that others would see it and think I was weak. I am ready now to surrender my right always to be strong. Amen."

As the days went by, the feeling of loneliness continued to be very real sometimes, but from the time of my en-

counter with Keilah I dealt with it in a different way. I tried
to remind myself of the reality of the Lord's presence and
to repeat His promise, "I am with you always, even unto
the end of the world." And at another depth, I no longer
tried always to appear strong. Not that I went around
inflicting my self-pity onto others, but I did allow myself
to be real. Keilah had seen me cry and had spoken truth
into my sorrow. Others would do so, too, I was certain.

Often as the months went by I was invited to the homes
of missionaries and enjoyed good meals and fellowship
with them. It disturbed me that I was not making many
contacts among the black African population. I did meet
African pastors now and then but most of the Africans I
saw were servants in the homes of my employer and my
new friends. It did not seem right to me that the Africans
waited on the white people who had come to this country
to serve them. I expressed as much in a letter home to
Hastings in England. "One thing I find very hard to get
used to," I wrote, "is having a black African servant, often
dressed in a smart white uniform, in contrast to the shabby
clothes he usually wears at other times during the day,
serve me at table. I keep wanting to get up and help him."
Sure that I would do things differently if as a white person
I had a position of authority in this newly independent
nation of blacks longing for "Africanization," I posted the
letter to England rather smugly.

Very quickly a reply came from Sylvia saying, "I and all
the family were delighted with the amazing change that
has come in you in that you want to get up and help the
Africans serve. You never wanted to help at home!" Her
remark was made in fun and I laughed as I pictured her face
as she wrote it. But it hit home. Even though she was
thousands of miles away, she had once again been used in
my life. I saw that I had a great deal to learn about servant-

BIRDVILLE
BAPTIST CHURCH
LIBRARY

hood and had by no means earned the right to criticize the relationship between blacks and whites and their service to each other. I needed to learn to serve in the capacity in which I had been placed here in Kenya. To my shame I knew that I was often far more concerned for my own comfort and happiness—as when I had struggled so with lonesomeness—than I was about learning how to serve.

During the coming months, either in the company of my old friends from St. Leonards Parish Church, or in that of new friends, I had the opportunity to make many weekend safaris to different parts of Kenya and to discover how limited my earlier dream had been of staying right at home in England. God knew me better than I knew myself and did not allow that provincialism to stay in place. Once I surrendered my right to live near what was known and comfortable, He opened to me astonishing glimpses of His creativity.

One weekend, for instance, was spent in Mombasa and I had my first view of the Indian Ocean, sparkling like a sapphire, its beaches fringed with palm trees. Borrowing snorkeling equipment I swam underwater in a warm and shallow coral reef and saw marine life I never knew existed. Brightly colored fish flashed to and fro against a background of white sand, shells, and pink coral in the enchanting, silent world under the water.

Journeys northwest of Nairobi took me to Lake Nakuru, which from a distance seemed to be pink. Closer examination revealed millions of flamingos covering the surface of the lake. One of the most awe-inspiring sights for me was the huge Rift Valley. I tried to describe it in letters home, but words could not capture its size and powerful majesty.

On another weekend, in the company of some friends visiting from England, I ventured, as inexperienced as my two companions, into a large game park in a rather ramshackle vehicle. We saw, close up, elephants, hunch-backed vultures, lions, rhinos, giraffes, cheetahs, and a variety of wonderful birds, the comical secretary bird, so named for the quill-like feather on his head, being one of the most entertaining. There were delicate-looking ga-zelle, ever watchful for predators, sheltering from the intense heat under sparse thorn trees. We delighted in our adventure, even surviving the changing of a flat tire miles away from civilization and help. *Can this really be me?* I asked myself as I lay under the mosquito netting on my bed in the little huts where we spent the night in the middle of the game reserve, listening to a rustling overhead. Bats! I was glad for the protective netting.

Being in this large, beautiful, and wild country was not only stretching me physically, but also mentally and spir-itually. I was developing "muscles" I did not know I had. If I had been able to look into the future I would have seen that the tasks in the years ahead needed this kind of prep-aration.

One weekend Archbishop and Mrs. Beecher invited me to accompany them on a safari to a village of the Masai tribe, where many had become Christians. They had built a church and had asked the Archbishop to dedicate it. I agreed to go with much excitement. It seemed that I did not have much opportunity to get to know many Africans, so here was a good chance to be with them. I knew that although the Archbishop and his wife did not speak Masai, some of the people would be fluent in Swahili and they would be able to communicate in that language. I hoped that in some way I, too, would be able to communicate with them.

Our journey to the Masai village meant a descent into the Rift Valley in the Archbishop's jeep. The lower we drove, the hotter it became. The jeep's windows were open (I had never seen a vehicle in Kenya with air-conditioning) and clouds of dry *murram*, the familiar red earth, rose behind our back wheels, some of it coming into the vehicle. The landscape became more and more inhospitable, rocky and arid. I could not imagine how people could live in such heat. The Masai, I had heard, were tall, slender, and strong. They were renowned warriors and made their living mainly on cattle. Now and then, in the distance, I saw a tall man with a red loincloth, staff in hand, herding a few scraggy cows. Nowhere did I see any water, but Mrs. Beecher explained that they knew exactly where to find water holes.

She also went on to tell me that the Masai have a very simple diet. Animal blood and milk were allowed to curdle together in gourds and this provided their main source of food. She told me that the medical profession had noted that the Masai tribe in general was not nearly as susceptible as other peoples to cardiovascular disease.

I shuddered, hoping that some other form of refreshment would be offered by the Masai to their visitors today. I remembered, however, that missionaries, in order to identify with the people with whom they were working, often bravely swallowed strange foods so as not to offend their hosts. I had recently heard the story of a worker in the Middle East who, seated with a group of Arabs, was offered what her hosts considered the choice part of the repast, a whole, cooked sheep's eye. She prayed, took it with thanks, and swallowed it. I wondered if I would have been as brave. Perhaps I would be faced with a chance to find out. It would be a good test to see how real was my desire to identify with the Africans.

The journey across the hot and dusty plain continued until we saw a village settlement and the Archbishop indicated that this was our destination. Alighting from the jeep we were greeted by Masai in their red loincloths, long-limbed and with noble faces. They were happy to see us and there was a festive atmosphere. Leading us through a scattering of huts, they proudly showed us the new brick church, which the Archbishop had come to dedicate. Very lean chickens hastened clucking out of our way and there seemed to be quite a few animals either behind fences or wandering in the dusty street. And then I saw something that sent a shiver down my spine. It was a goat, clearly dead but also very recently dead. I knew that by the twitching of a couple of its limbs. And what was that bowl doing near its neck? Was this how the Masai obtained their gory diet, from the jugular veins of animals?

It did not take long to find out. Walking in the wake of Archbishop and Mrs. Beecher, who were conversing in Swahili with a couple of Masai leaders, I met the eye of a Masai over to my left. He smiled at me and looked down at the bowl he was holding. It was full of fresh blood. Raising it toward his lips he made a motion as if he were about to drink it, then handed it to me with an enquiring look and a similar motion. I felt my stomach turn and many questions went through my head rapidly. If I followed the example of most intrepid missionaries I would take it and drink some, trusting the Lord that somehow I would be enabled to swallow it. If I did not I might run the risk of hurting his feelings.

But equally rapidly I made up my mind. "No, thank you," I said. He grinned broadly, and suddenly surprised me by saying in English, "I did not expect that you wanted it." With relief I learned that he had had the advantage (one of the few in his area) of a good education and knew how Europeans felt about his tribe's diet. He had just been joking with me and I did not need to worry that he had been offended!

I reflected on the incident when, after the church dedication and fruit, tea, and bread refreshments, the jeep began to climb back out of the Rift Valley leaving behind another trail of red dust. My conclusion was that although I often made things difficult for myself by anticipating that the very hardest things would be asked of me, in fact those things hardly ever happened. Even this afternoon I had not had a serious request to eat Masai food. The bowl had been offered to me as a joke by an educated Masai. Neither he nor the Lord had expected me to drink its contents. If the future was to hold times when I would need to identify with Christians in ways difficult for me, I was sure the Lord would give grace for those times. I had a fleeting sense that the future would indeed require a much deeper and longer identification with some of God's people than had been required in those few hours with the Masai in Kenya.

As 1967 progressed, I knew that I was growing. Coming to Kenya had opened up not just a different place of work. It had opened my mind and expanded it. England was not the center of the world. Kenya was equally important and beyond her borders was a whole world in need. There was so much to do and financial resources were small. I was amazed at the very small budget on which the Church of the Province of East Africa operated. The people who, it seemed to me, were the most generous in providing financial aid were the Americans. Often letters arrived from the United States containing checks. I thought I would like to know more about that country and wondered if any future travels would include a visit to the United States.

As my year in Kenya wore on, the Archbishop asked if I would revise my plan to leave and invited me to stay on at his office. Knowing that a full-time secretary was coming from England to help him, and wanting to keep to the original one-year plan, I declined his offer. I was hoping that a different area of service might open up for me, perhaps, for example, as a teacher.

That the Lord had a different way for me I had no way of knowing. What a strange coincidence that I heard hints of my future twice in one evening and never knew it.

That evening I went to a meeting held in a large home in one of the suburbs of Nairobi where Christians from various churches in the town came together regularly for fellowship and prayer.

The meeting began with energetic singing and there was an unusual sense of the presence of God. I gave myself to the worship and listened quietly to the testimonies that followed, still far too shy about speaking in public to think of adding my voice to the accounts of God's faithfulness.

Then came the time usually reserved for prayer and a young man asked for prayer for Christians suffering for their faith in Russia and Eastern Europe. He went on to tell a tale about a Dutchman who had prayed to God, asking what he could do to relieve their situation. God had directed the Dutchman to go to Moscow with Bibles, giving him an assurance that he would know to whom he was to give them, although he did not have a name or address. At the same time that the Dutchman prayed, God spoke to a Russian Christian in Siberia whose church of 150 had no Bible. In answer to his prayer God told the Russian Christian that he should go to Moscow where he would find a Bible for his church. So it was that the Dutchman traveled two thousand miles from the west, somehow crossing the Russian border with contraband Bibles, and the Russian traveled two thousand miles from the east. The two of them met up in Moscow and the Dutchman handed over to his Russian brother the Bibles he had brought.

As the young man told that story in the quiet Nairobi suburb with the crickets chirping outside and the delightful scent of frangipani stealing through the open windows, I became aware that I was listening not just politely, but with a deep and passionate interest. Never had I known that Russian Christians were denied Bibles. And I had never heard that God and His people would go to such lengths to make sure Bibles were provided. The Dutchman's name was a strange one. Brother Andrew. I wondered if he were a monk.

And then, as the requests for prayer continued, I found myself hearing another strange name. Prayer was asked for a certain Corrie ten Boom. She had just come to Uganda where she was to spend a year's sabbatical. Corrie ten Boom was described as a lady of rather ample girth who had no real home. She traveled the world constantly, and had done so since the 1940s, telling anybody who would listen all she had learned about the love of God while in a concentration camp in Nazi Germany.

For some reason, I found myself listening to the story about Corrie ten Boom with as much interest as I had had for the story about the Bibles to Russia. Everybody in the room seemed to have heard of Corrie and to have deep respect for her. It seemed she was something of a legend. I thought I could learn much from her and wondered if she had written a book about her experiences. If so, perhaps I could read it someday.

My time in Kenya drew to a close. It was a sad day for me when I stood in the circle of flowers at Bishopsbourne and took my leave of the staff including Archbishop and Mrs. Beecher, and of still-frowning, wonderful old Keilah. Waving, I headed away from this lovely wild country and boarded a boat in Mombasa. I had decided that a return to Europe by boat would be much more interesting than the relatively short plane journey, especially since the recent war in the Middle East had closed the Suez Canal and the quickest water route to Europe was now around South Africa and the Cape of Good Hope.

During the three-week sea voyage, when very few stops were made, I had plenty of time to reflect on the past year. I knew that I was a different person from the one who had arrived in East Africa from England just thirteen months before. I had been challenged mentally, physically, and spiritually, but God had not let me down. He had helped me meet the challenges, including loneliness and cultural differences. I remembered how I had been reluctant to commit my life to Him for fear His will might take me to work outside England. His will had indeed required that, but even after one short year I could see that I had gained more than I had ever given and my life had been immeasurably enriched. What was more, I was finding the fulfillment of a deep sense of adventure I never knew I had.

The ocean liner made its way through warm tropical seas to the cold and rough waters of Europe, docking in a frigid Brindisi in northern Italy. From there I had to take a train to a northern French port in order to catch the ferry to Dover. The English Channel was the roughest I had ever known it on that Christmas Eve in 1967 as I prepared to meet my family whom I knew would be waiting on the dock. I could not wait to tell them, especially Sylvia, some of the things I had learned, particularly how God had taken my fear of leaving England and had turned it into great satisfaction. I remembered the hymn I had sung as a child and whose words I had resisted—

> *Hast thou not seen how thy desires e'er have been*
> *granted in what he ordaineth?*

I was beginning to see it.

Chapter Four

'Welkom in Holland'

Back in the little red-brick house at the main gates of Alexandra Park that Christmas in 1967, there would never be enough time to tell my parents, Sylvia, and Digger all that had happened to me in Kenya. How could I describe the grandeur of the country and explain the changes that were taking place in me?

And I was not the only one who had undergone changes. I wanted to hear all about Sylvia's adventures at the University of Sussex and about my brother's plans. Digger had left grammar school and had taken a gardening job while he decided what he wanted to specialize in for a future career. Mother continued to work long hours at the local hospital and Dad was still busy at the Parks Department office.

No wonder I loved home! Typical of every Christmas in our family, this year's festival was full of warmth, color, and simple gifts. Our Christmas Day meal was the traditional turkey, pork, and chippolata sausages, Brussels sprouts, roast potatoes, and stuffing. As if that were not enough, it was followed by Christmas pudding, a heavy, dark fruit dessert, over which brandy was poured and lighted before it was carried, immersed for a short while in blue flame, to the dining room table. Following tradition, too, we pulled our brightly colored paper crackers. These contained mottos, colored paper hats, and small games. We donned the hats and read the mottos and laughed and reminisced by the fire. Time always stood still at Christmas.

But the day was all too soon over. The color and warmth of the Christmas season vanished in the biting, gray days of early January. The rest of the family returned to studies and work and I started again to think about my own future. What was to happen next?

Since Kenya I was still thinking of changing my secretarial line of work, perhaps going into teaching. There was no teacher training college in Hastings. Several friends were living in Bristol, in the west of England, where there were seminaries and a university. I decided to go to Bristol, apply for work and investigate teacher training in the area. So, at the end of February 1968, I found work as secretary to the matron of the Royal Hospital for Sick Children.

How frequently, it seemed—once I had surrendered my rights to self-determination—did the Lord guide me into His will for my life by apparently accidental meetings and events. I came to know a young teacher, Margaret White, who was looking for a roommate. She and I shared a comfortable flat about a mile from the hospital. And, almost as "coincidentally," it seemed at first, on my daily walk to and from the office, I passed an old building that bore a plaque stating that this was one of George Muller's orphanages. I recognized Muller's name as a man of great faith who had sheltered and fed orphans in Bristol during the previous century. Each time I saw the plaque I was challenged to have faith in God. It was a timely reminder, for from the first I seemed to be floundering.

My work as secretary to the matron quickly proved to be

extremely tedious, after my year in the always different world of Kenya. Mainly I sat alone in a small office typing laundry lists and letters to prospective nurses. Was I in the right place? The idea of becoming a teacher was not forming in my mind in any compelling way. Had I made a mistake coming to Bristol?

Now and then I would escape the confines of the little office and enter a maze of corridors. Various wards held children of all ages, some recovering from minor illness, others terminally ill. It helped to see the children I was assisting indirectly by typing laundry lists. But the lack of fulfillment persisted and so far I did not know what to do about it. Guidance just would not come. . . .

After I had been in Bristol for a couple of months I was introduced to a young man called John, a theological student at one of Bristol's seminaries. We went out together several times and I had to wonder whether or not marriage was, at last, now part of God's plan. How I hoped it was. Then I need not be concerned about an uncertain work future for I would be raising a family and helping John in his work. For several weeks we met and then John graduated. He accepted the curacy of a church in a far-away town. When he left Bristol he said only that he'd enjoyed knowing me! It was clear that he wanted to end the friendship.

I was disappointed, not just that I had lost John, but that God was apparently silent. It had not been like this before when I asked for guidance. Why was I here and where was I going? One morning as I passed the George Muller orphanage I found inspiration in his great faith. Muller, I'd read, was always surrendered in his prayers, trusting only in God and not in his own understanding. Had my idea of becoming a teacher been my own understanding?

I decided to talk to the Lord about my needs in a very definite way.

The hospital property contained a small chapel that I liked to visit. It was rather dark, but very quiet, and one lunchtime, rather than join other staff in the noisy canteen, I made my way to the chapel.

Seated on an oak bench, I reviewed the situation. This was early summer of 1968, more than three years since my life-changing encounter with the Lord at Ashburnham, and although I had experienced His help and guidance during those years, He seemed so silent now. I searched my heart to see if I knew about any sin that could be hindering my receiving God's guidance. Of course there was sin that needed forgiveness every day, but I could think of nothing I had not confessed.

I therefore decided that the best thing to do was to make another surrender to God of the right to my own will. In that little dark chapel I prayed something like this: "Lord God, You have guided me so clearly in the past. When I went to Africa I trusted in the fact that, just as You promise in Your Word, You have good works prepared for me to walk in. I am discontented where I am now, typing laundry lists, but I come to You and I surrender that discontent. If You want me to do this kind of work forever, I will. Please make me willing." And then came the part of the prayer that, even as I prayed it, inspired new faith in me: "It seems that marriage is not in Your plan for now. I surrender that anew too, even though I am twenty-four and that seems so old to be single. But, Father, if marriage is not Your plan, will You please give me an exciting and adventurous life?"

When I finished my prayer, I walked back to my office slowly. There was a sense of anticipation that had not been there before, a conviction that God would indeed answer the prayer for adventure. I had received that faith only after making a renewed surrender of my will. So, I thought, as I sat down in front of my typewriter for the afternoon's work, one of the keys to receiving guidance is to *keep my heart in an attitude of real surrender.*

It was amazing how I had changed, I thought, as I walked home that evening. The reticent me of three years ago would never have asked for excitement and adventure. Perhaps it had been necessary for me to take this dull job to see that I was a different person now. What would happen next?

A few weeks later, my flatmate, Margaret, told me that she was going to spend a week of her summer vacation at a Christian conference center in Matlock in the county of Derbyshire. I had heard of Matlock, situated in the beautiful English Peak District just about in the center of England. "Why don't you come along?" she said. "It will be a Dutch/English missionary week and there are some good speakers." She explained that the conference would be made up of an approximately equal number of Dutch and English participants and that the main speakers were two people called Brother Andrew and Corrie ten Boom.

At the names, I felt interest stirring. Where had I heard them before? Then I knew. I remembered the evening meeting of Christians in Nairobi, with the scent of frangipani stealing through the windows and the chirping of crickets outside. There I had heard the names of these two people and learned about their work. What a coincidence! Immediately I agreed to go.

My work at the hospital continued to be unfulfilling and I knew, because of the lack of peace in my heart, that I should submit my notice, accompany Margaret to the missionary week and trust God for whatever developed after that. So it was that, at the end of July 1968, I resigned my job and in the first week of August caught a train to Matlock, which is a journey of several hours from the south coast. When the train arrived at the small station I found the platform filled with tall, large-boned, mainly blond, laughing, and noisy people. They were speaking in a language that, at first hearing, seemed to have some rather ugly gutteral sounds. The main impression, though, was that these people laughed a lot. It was my first contact with the Dutch.

Quite unlike my shy self at the time, I introduced myself to one of the quieter ones. She could speak English well and told me that her name was Marijke. She introduced me to a friend of hers whose name I liked immediately, Riska. About my age with dark hair, gold-rimmed glasses, and a very vivacious personality, Riska told me that she worked in a town in The Netherlands with the strange name of Harderwijk.

After a short wait on the platform of the train station we were transported through very hilly and beautiful scenery to a large old house. I was ushered with my suitcase to a very plain dormitory containing six bunkbeds and a couple of built-in closets. The bathroom was at the end of the corridor.

After freshening up, I made my way to the dining room. There was a lot of noise. Although there was an equal number of English and Dutch participants, the presence of the Dutch was far more noticeable. I had not realized that they were such a boisterous people. They made me feel even more conscious of my own shyness and I hoped I could manage to hold my own with them. I realized I was a little afraid of them and then chided myself for being foolish. After all, this was only for five days.

Soon after supper we all assembled in the main meeting room of the conference center, almost as plainly furnished as the dining room and dormitory. It was a large room in the front of the house and the approximately one hundred of us found seats on a variety of unmatching chairs. Brother Andrew was to be tonight's speaker. Why did he have such a strange name? I was curious to know what he looked like.

I did not have to wait long to find out. Soon a slender, brown-haired, middle-aged man of medium height with a thin and intelligent face was introduced. So this was Brother Andrew. He explained that he was not a monk and that the reason for his abbreviated name had to do with the safety of Eastern European Christians. He had recently authored a book in English called *God's Smuggler* that told how for the past thirteen years he had smuggled Bibles into Iron Curtain countries. He did not want his real name to appear on the book and possibly endanger those he had visited. And, he said, his Dutch first name would be hard to pronounce in English. His own English was excellent, his speaking style commanding.

Next he said something rather alarming. "We are going to be together for almost a week," he began. "So we had better get to know each other. I want each of you to stand, to say your name, what your work is, and why you have come."

I felt my heart thumping. I still had a dread of speaking in public—even with such a simple task as Brother Andrew was requesting. And besides, how could I answer him since I did not have a job and did not really know why I was here? Perhaps I would be overlooked. I was near the back, and Brother Andrew might not see me.

During the next few minutes, delegates answered the questions with interesting variety, their information often cleverly formulated. I admired the Dutch for their good use of English. They all seemed to know each other although they came from different churches. Several missionaries, pastors, teachers, and students were present. Almost shaking with anxiety as my turn came closer, I tried without success to concentrate on the information being given.

All too soon it was my turn. Rising, I rushed through the words I had rehearsed: "My-name-is-Pamela-Rosewell-and-I-am-an-unemployed-secretary-and-I-came -here-because-I-want-to-learn-more-about-missionary - work." Then I sat down. Happily no one asked me to elaborate.

After each delegate had had a chance to introduce himself or herself, Brother Andrew launched into a dramatic and compelling message. He told how God had led him, thirteen years earlier, to begin a ministry to Christians in Russia, Eastern Europe, and other Communist countries. He called them "the suffering Church" and illustrated his talk with many examples of how God had worked miracles in order to allow Bibles and help to cross Communist borders.

I listened to Brother Andrew's talk with attention. His story held me and I found myself identifying with those in Communist countries who are denied Bibles.

The next morning, to my surprise, I was approached by one of the conference leaders who told me that Brother Andrew would like to speak to me during a free hour that afternoon and we arranged that I would meet with him at two o'clock.

When the time arrived, Brother Andrew explained that he had been interested to hear me say that I was an unemployed secretary. Would I be willing to help him with some correspondence? I agreed, and spent several free hours typing letters.

Brother Andrew was not the only speaker. He introduced us to the lady I had heard about in Africa, the one who seemed to be a legend in her lifetime, Corrie ten Boom. She was silver-haired and in her youth had been a tall woman, probably my own height of five feet seven inches. Now she was stooped and appeared shorter. I was struck by the energy she conveyed in her strong build and determined jaw.

Corrie ten Boom had recently accompanied Brother Andrew on a visit to Vietnam. I was impressed that somebody 77 years old would undertake such a dangerous and tiring journey. She was known as "Tante" Corrie by the Dutch (*tante* was their word for "Aunt") and the English delegates soon adopted that title for her. She spoke to us not just about Vietnam, but about imprisonment in a concentration camp during the last World War, emphasizing the necessity of forgiving our enemies. When she was not speaking, Tante Corrie seemed to be surrounded always by groups of people wanting to talk to her. I wished I could meet her, too, but felt in awe of her and that I had no reason to take any of her time.

And there was another speaker whose story added flesh-and-blood reality to Corrie ten Boom's and Brother Andrew's challenges. Ildiko was Hungarian, here from her Iron Curtain country on a short visa. She walked onto the platform one morning, a strong-featured girl with light brown hair dressed in a pale pink twinset and woollen skirt. There were dark circles under her eyes. Ildiko brought Hungary to life . . . the depressed atmosphere in the beautiful city of Budapest where she lived, the hard factory work from dawn to dusk, the persecution of her family because they were Christians, the clandestine meetings, and the secret arrival of Bibles from the West. In addition to her own work with local Christians, Ildiko was also concerned about those in foreign countries who did not know Christ. "I find it very hard to get up at five o'clock in the morning," she said, "but when I think of all the people in China who have never heard the Gospel, I do get up. I ask God to change the situation there."

During one of my typing sessions Brother Andrew told me that his recently published book *God's Smuggler* had caused a great increase in his English correspondence. "I wonder if you are God's answer to my prayers for an English secretary," he said. "Will you come to Holland and help us?"

His directness startled me. Most of the Dutch seemed to be direct, in contrast to the more circumspect British. But at least you knew exactly where you were with the Dutch.

I told Brother Andrew I would think it over and let him know before the end of the conference. It was an intriguing invitation. I believed very strongly in his message about the suffering Church. However, starting back in Nairobi, I was sure of one thing: I did not want another secretarial job. *But then who am I*, I thought, *to insist that I be free to choose what I am to do?* Ildiko would have jumped at the chance of helping the suffering Church, but her temporary visa would expire soon and she would have to return to Hungary.

What was there to lose, I decided, in going to Holland on a short-term basis? After prayer I resolved to tell Brother Andrew that I would join him for a few weeks before starting what I hoped would be a new direction in the Lord's service. He agreed to this.

I next discovered that Riska, the dark-haired Dutch girl I had met at the train station, would also shortly be joining Brother Andrew and his wife, Corry, to help with their children (a fifth baby was soon to be born) and to assist in the office. She told me that her landlady had an extra room in the house where she lived in the town of Harderwijk and she knew I would be welcome there. Brother Andrew's house and office were in the next town, Ermelo, and I could get there each day by bus.

Fascinated by the new unfolding adventure, I returned to Hastings to pack my bags.

If my family had any misgivings about my undertaking to help a mysterious Dutch missionary, they did not show them. They accompanied me to Dover to catch the ferry and for the second time in less than two years I said goodbye to home and England, a freedom I'd not have imagined possible before I began this adventure in surrendered rights.

During the long Channel crossing to Belgium and subsequent train journey I tried to recall all I had learned in school about Holland. I remembered that large areas of the country had been won from the sea and that she had once been a great sea power. Amazing, for such a small land. I knew, too, that Holland had a strong chemical and agricultural industry and had in previous centuries produced influential painters. My impression, probably gained from the paintings, was that Holland was quiet, rural, and not much involved in the rush of modern Europe.

As soon as the train crossed the Dutch border, however, I saw that my vague impression was false. Here was a fast-moving, efficient, very modern nation. As the train made its way through The Netherlands, it passed large towns with new buildings. The main cities were linked by high-speed freeways. There was a large amount of agricultural land, but building work had clearly been planned so that it did not encroach too much upon the countryside.

Flat, bright green pastureland interspersed with rows of poplar trees stretched into the distance where often a church tower indicated a small town or village. Town and country were consistently clean and neat. I noticed that the houses had large front windows and that the Dutch kept their drapes drawn back, inviting me to look through sparkling windowpanes into their living rooms, all of which seemed to have a great number of potted plants. This display of openness seemed to tally with the directness I had noted in the Dutch at the conference in England. It endeared me to them. I felt welcome.

And then there was the light. I had noticed it immediately on entering Holland. There was a certain brightness to the light I had not noticed on any of my travels thus far. What was the explanation? Was it perhaps that Holland's sky, in the absence of mountains, was much larger than in most countries? I did not know. But I did like this country. The beautiful light had a comforting effect on me. It reminded me of the presence of God.

Changing trains at Utrecht was not as difficult as I had imagined it would be in a country where I could not speak the language. I discovered that most of the Dutch seemed to speak English and they helped me find the train to Ermelo, a small town in the center of The Netherlands. Brother Andrew was waiting for me at the railway station in a large gray French station wagon. *"Welkom in Holland, Pam,"* were his first words. I was relieved to see him. He told me that he would look forward to my starting in the office in the morning. In the meantime, though, he would show me where I was to work and live for the next few weeks.

Driving through quiet streets and a busy main road, Brother Andrew turned in at the driveway of a three-story house with a sloping roof and a separate garage on the right-hand side. This, he told me, was where he and his family lived. Inside I was welcomed by his wife, Corry, and their four children. Then he took me to the third story of the house, an attic room under the eaves of the sloping roof. It contained four desks with office chairs, several typewriters and a few filing cabinets. The garage and another storage place nearby contained boxes of Bibles in the languages of Eastern Europe, Brother Andrew explained. I listened carefully and did not say much. The adventure was deepening. Was a dangerous international ministry really being conducted from an attic and garage in this quiet Dutch town?

My short introduction to his family and work completed, Brother Andrew presented me with a signed copy of his book *God's Smuggler*. I would need to read it quickly, I thought, if I was going to start work in the office the next day. I knew so little about what was going on.

We got back into the gray station wagon and I began to realize why Brother Andrew's car was so large. This must be one of the vehicles used to take Bibles to Eastern Europe. He took me on a ten-minute journey to the city of Harderwijk, situated on the old Zuiderzee, now an inland lake called the Ijsselmeer, and delivered me to a little terraced house near the harbor. Here Riska, my dark-haired, vivacious Dutch friend, had rooms. She was waiting to receive me and introduce me to Juffrouw de Graaf, her elderly, white-haired landlady who greeted me with a firm handshake and a flood of Dutch not a word of which I understood except *Welkom*.

Next I was shown the spare bedroom at the back of the house. It was small and peaceful with white walls and paintwork and a white counterpane on the bed. This was to be my home during my weeks in Holland. As soon as supper was over I retreated to my little white refuge, unpacked my suitcase, prepared for the night and got into bed. It had been a long day and I was tired, but I needed at least to start reading *God's Smuggler*.

As I entered the world described in the book, it became increasingly hard to leave it. I read about God's call on Brother Andrew's life and about his willingness to risk that life to help those suffering for their faith. I went in imagination to Eastern Europe, felt the confinement of the Communist system, and identified with the Christians in their need of help. I saw in my mind many Christians like the tired-eyed Ildiko getting up at five o'clock for prayer and paying the price each day for following Christ.

I was so glad I had come to Holland. A deep sense of satisfaction filled me before I finally slept that night in Miss de Graaf's quiet white room. I resolved to do my best to make these few short weeks that I had agreed to come to Holland count for the sake of those suffering for Christ. I did not know that their cause would so grip me that it would never let me go.

Chapter Five

Behind the Iron Curtain

During the next days I became deeply immersed in a busy and mysterious new world. With me were two full-time co-workers, blond young men called Leen and Goos. (Riska was to join the work in a few months' time.) One of the first challenges was to learn how to say Goos's name. The G was pronounced with a hard fricative produced in the throat, the double *o* as in *rose,* but much further back in the mouth, and the *s* was a sharp one. I despaired of ever saying the name correctly. Leen and Goos were high-spirited and cheerful and they carried on their business mainly in Dutch. Soon, from the jumble of new sounds, I began to pick out a word: *reis,* "journey." Leen and Goos spent much of their time planning journeys to Eastern Europe.

There was no time to get too curious, though, because I had my hands full with my own work. On my desk were piles of letters mainly from the United States. Most were responses from readers of *God's Smuggler.* My main task, explained Brother Andrew, was to keep the English correspondence up-to-date. Some readers wanted to know how they could support the work financially, others wanted more information for prayer. Many, impressed by the specific guidance they had read about in the book, asked how they too could receive definite guidance from God. And some, in deep grief, through difficult personal circumstances, asked for help and prayer.

At first Brother Andrew dictated the replies; then, as I became more familiar with the work, he asked me to formulate answers for his signature, occasionally giving requested information on behalf of the work over my own signature. I could see through this, and the way he allowed Leen and Goos to plan journeys to Eastern Europe, that he was a man who wanted his co-workers to take responsibility. I was honored that he would allow me such freedom. It helped me gain confidence and seek the Lord earnestly for the right answers to the often difficult questions contained in the letters arriving daily in the little attic office.

I began to see that the suffering church in Eastern Europe was unconsciously involved in a ministry of its own. The story of their bravery and suffering was helping Christians in the free and prosperous West. I wondered if I would ever have the opportunity to visit an Iron Curtain country. Already, in just ten days of working with Brother Andrew, Christians behind the Iron Curtain seemed much nearer. It was more than the fact that I was in continental Europe with no channel dividing us.

And then on August 21, 1968, the Soviet Union and her Warsaw Pact allies invaded Czechoslovakia in the night. We watched on television as Russian tanks rolled into Prague and found ourselves identifying strongly with the Czech Christians who had thought that under Dubcek, their new leader, greater freedom lay ahead. Instead they were suddenly confronted with the deposing of Dubcek and the prospect of a future under even closer Soviet domination.

Brother Andrew moved quickly. He canceled all plans and got ready to go to Czechoslovakia to bring what help and encouragement he could. Packing his large gray station wagon he left, alone, within a few hours.

The fact that this tragic international event had happened during my short stay in Holland impressed me deeply. Could it be that the Lord was telling me that He was offering me an opportunity to help the suffering Church for longer than my planned few weeks? Brother Andrew must have found it easier to leave knowing that I and the other office staff could deal with questions and correspondence during his absence.

After a few days, Brother Andrew returned bearing up-to-date information about the state of the Czech Church, the courage of the Czech people, and their need for Bibles, literature, and practical help. Activity in our attic office accelerated as Leen and Goos prepared copy for a special edition of the letter sent regularly to prayer supporters. Work piled up. I hardly had to pray about staying on. It seemed the obvious thing to do. As soon as possible I approached Brother Andrew about it and he accepted my offer with obvious gratitude but also in the unceremonious way I now knew was typical of the Dutch.

So it was that in the early autumn of 1968 I returned to Hastings to pack my belongings for a longer stay in Holland. I worked quickly, wanting to get back to The Netherlands with the least possible delay. What a contrast with my tedious work at the children's hospital in Bristol! But if I had not gone to Bristol I would not so quickly have had a new experience with surrendering my rights . . . and all that swiftly followed Margaret's invitation to the missionary week. My meeting with Brother Andrew. My heartfelt involvement with the suffering Church. The ministry in Holland was one of the good works the Lord had beforehand prepared for me. I was sure of it. Resurrendering my "right" to my own will had released God's guidance to that work.

On the Saturday after my arrival back in Holland, Riska suggested that we go to hear Corrie ten Boom speak at a nearby missionary conference. I agreed readily. I might even have an opportunity to meet Tante Corrie! Perhaps this time I'd not be as reticent as I had been at the Matlock conference.

Sure enough, at the end of the meeting Riska found a chance to introduce me to Tante Corrie and to her tall, blonde companion, Ellen de Kroon. *How challenging Ellen's job must be,* I thought fleetingly.

But my real attention was on Tante Corrie. She was wearing a blue dress and jacket and her silver-gray hair was drawn back and up and secured in a roll. Her skin was a healthy olive with a hint of a tan, but it was her eyes that particularly impressed me. They were clear and blue and discerning. Perhaps it was fanciful, but it seemed to me that Tante Corrie took in not just my external features, but was able to see deeper, into my being. In any case I obviously had her full attention. She beamed when she heard I had come to help her friend Brother Andrew.

"Child," she said, in a clear alto voice, "we are so glad you have come to Holland. You are always welcome in my home. Please come and spend the night with us. Ellen and I want to get to know you."

I felt honored by her welcome, but a bit puzzled. Which home did she mean? Was she not usually traveling around the world? And had I not heard that she had sold the family watchshop and home in Haarlem many years before? As I thanked her, Tante Corrie's attention was claimed by somebody else wanting to speak to her and Ellen took over.

"Pam," Ellen said, "Tante Corrie will leave for the United States in a couple of weeks. Come to us next weekend. Riska will tell you how to get there."

Ellen spotted somebody near the door to whom she needed to speak, and excused herself but not before she added, "By the way, we don't have a guest bedroom, but Tante Corrie has an extra bed in her room. She will be glad to have you share with her."

On the way back to our digs in Harderwijk, Riska told me that Tante Corrie had been loaned an elegant apartment in the town of Soestdijk, which was her base when she was in Holland. The apartment owner was a Dutch baroness who lived and worked in Israel and the apartment complex stood next to the Queen of Holland, Queen Juliana's, palace. It sounded fascinating. I decided that I would like to take up Tante Corrie's invitation but anticipated it with some hesitation. The prospect of sharing a bedroom with Corrie ten Boom was rather daunting. I was in awe of her. There was an intense pureness about her. She must have an extraordinary walk with God. Probably she got up for prayer at four in the morning. What would she think of me when she found out that I did not?

The next Saturday, following Dutch custom to take flowers to your hostess, I made my way to Tante Corrie's borrowed apartment in Soestdijk and as soon as Ellen welcomed me inside and accepted my carnations with thanks, I found myself in a world the Dutch would describe as *gezellig*. I had already discovered that that word crops up many times daily in normal conversation. I had not been able to find an English equivalent, but had noticed it was used to describe situations of warmth, togetherness, fellowship, and relaxed atmosphere. I found this in abundance behind the front door of Tante Corrie's home. The warmth of the welcome and the acceptance

Tante Corrie gave me impressed me far more than the tastefully coordinated furnishings of her borrowed apartment, pleasing though they were.

She and Ellen were busy and I tried to make myself useful by correcting English copy for publication and typing some letters. The telephone rang often and there were some visitors. Tante Corrie received them all in a very relaxed way, giving them her full attention. I noticed that when she wanted to draw an interview to an end she suggested to the visitor that they now pray. It was a clear signal that the visitor's allotted time had come to a close and they took the hint. Before each visitor left, Tante Corrie handed him or her a signed copy of one of her books.

Often during the day, Tante Corrie stopped and asked the Lord for help with whatever matter had just cropped up—whether it was as a result of a phone call, visitor, letter, or plans for her forthcoming speaking in the United States. I was very impressed with the simple, immediate way in which she addressed the Lord. But I still wondered, as bedtime approached, how the night would be. From the books I had read it seemed that many leaders of her stature struggled in prayer for hours at night. Would she?

When bedtime came, Tante Corrie emerged from the bathroom wearing a pair of comfortable-looking warm pajamas, her silver-gray hair released from the roll and hanging to her shoulders. Without ceremony she climbed into bed, said, "Goodnight, child," and turned out the light. I slept rather fitfully and looked toward her sleeping form several times as the night wore on. There appeared to be no nocturnal prayer times. Or specially-set-aside early morning prayer time either. She slept soundly until the morning, rising at about 8 A.M. after Ellen had served her breakfast in bed.

As I puzzled a bit about this I realized that *all* of Corrie ten Boom's waking hours were a sort of ongoing prayer, which meant that isolated "times of prayer" were perhaps rare.

She got as much rest at night as she could because she needed her energy for the busy days. And during those busy days she went very often to the Lord in prayer, as naturally as if He were in the room with her. How I yearned to have that prayer relationship with God, too.

Sunday included worship in a nearby church, lunch at a pancake house deep in the woods, and an afternoon walk. In the late afternoon a group of young people arrived and after some fellowship and a sandwich supper Tante Corrie led in the playing of several games. The room was soon full of hilarity. I could not remember laughing so much in months. Tante Corrie frequently gave the impression that she was losing a particular game and then, somehow, came through and beat the rest of us.

Before I left to return to Harderwijk, Tante Corrie told me about a project she clearly found very exciting. It seemed that there was a book about her life being written on her behalf by two authors, a husband-and-wife team called John and Elizabeth Sherrill. I recognized their names as the co-authors of Brother Andrew's book. Tante Corrie told me that the Sherrills would be in The Netherlands soon and that she would need help with the transcribing of some taped interviews for the new book. Its title was to be *The Hiding Place*. Would I be willing to help with the typing? I told her I would be.

On my way home I reviewed the unusual weekend. Tante Corrie had not been what I expected. Although she had not lost her aura of true purity, she had turned out to be so normal! She did not spend long hours in closeted prayer, she had a very cozy and welcoming home, and she was tremendous fun. I remembered how in Africa when I had first heard of Corrie ten Boom I wondered if she had written a book about her experiences. I could never have foreseen then that I would be asked by her to help in the preparing for publication of her life's story.

The autumn of 1968 passed into winter and Riska joined the work full-time to help in the office and with Brother Andrew and Corry's children. They had just become the parents of their fifth child, a little girl. Shortly afterward Brother Andrew moved his family to a house in Harder-wijk, where I lived. This time the office, although nearby, was separate from the family home. Riska moved to an apartment nearer work and I took over her two rooms on the second floor of the little terraced house near the harbor. I also joined millions of Dutch people in choosing a bicycle as my main mode of transport to and from work and stores.

The office was becoming increasingly busy. More and more requests for help were reaching us from Eastern Europe. Co-workers Leen and Goos made many journeys there and they also trained volunteers to help carry Bibles to the Soviet Union, Romania, Hungary, Czechoslovakia, Bulgaria, East Germany, and Yugoslavia. Such was the increase in the amount of work that two more cars were added to the ministry. As each team returned telling of yet another successful crossing with contraband literature, I felt a growing respect for the ministry and Brother Andrew's leadership and faith.

I will never forget the day Brother Andrew himself had to give up one of his most treasured "rights," to visit personally the believers behind the Iron Curtain. When he told us about his decision I saw in his eyes just how much this conclusion was costing him. But, he said, because his name had become so well-known it was best for the safety of the believers if he put an end to his East European journeys. With typical determination he turned his attention to a country many said was impossible to penetrate: Red China, with its so-called Bamboo Curtain. I was learning that part of Brother Andrew's calling was to challenge Christians to have faith that there are no closed doors for the Gospel.

In the spring of 1969 I underwent a challenge of my own. A special journey was being planned to Czechoslovakia in order to take advantage of an important European event. The finalists for the European Football Cup were the soccer teams of Ajax, Amsterdam (the Dutch team), and Spartak, Trnava (the Slovak team). The final was to be played in Trnava in eastern Czechoslovakia. Leen came up with the idea that two carloads of people visit Czechoslovakia, ostensibly as soccer fans, but also bearing very important hidden cargo. Riska and I were invited to be part of the girls' team in one of the cars, the gray Opel station wagon.

While I longed to take this opportunity to look behind the mysterious borders of Eastern Europe, I was also fearful. Czechoslovakia was one of the harder countries in which to work. Soviet troops were still there. I had seen many returning teams and knew how rough it could be for people in Czechoslovakia who were at odds with the government. I knew God worked miracles to get Bibles and Christian books across the borders. But would He do so if there was not total faith in my heart? There was certainly a little faith, but there was fear, too, even after prayer for guidance.

There was not much time to waver. If I was to go with the others I needed to submit my passport to the Czech embassy in The Hague for a visa. I decided to do it. If Brother Andrew could give up his right to visit Christians behind the Iron Curtain I could in a small way take his place! If it were not God's plan for me to go, He would show me. In the meantime, while waiting for the visas, we ostensible fans of Ajax Amsterdam Football Club made ready for the journey, packing whistles and noisemakers and other items that would be a normal part of a soccer fan's luggage. The two cars were packed with help for the Czech Christians—Bibles, Christian literature, clothes, and items of food that were scarce in their country, such as coffee.

The visa came through. So, early on a dull and windy day in mid-April, two cars left the Dutch base heading for the German border and the autobahn leading to Austria. At first we traveled in convoy and then, at one of the rest stops, agreed to go our own way and to meet each other again late that night in a village near Salzburg in Austria where we were to spend the night. Four of us—Riska, two other Dutch girls, and I—shared the driving as we traveled down West Germany's fast-moving freeway. In high spirits the four of us sang and talked and joked our way through hundreds of miles of autobahn. I wished I could keep up with the conversation but just seven months after my arrival in Holland, I was not yet fluent in Dutch.

Late that night we crossed the German-Austrian border. Following directions on a hand-drawn map we drove into a quiet village near the town of Salzburg and found our way to a large chalet where the other car was waiting. A few minutes later, very tired, I sank into a comfortable Austrian bed under an eiderdown.

Early the next morning when I looked through the window onto a sun-splashed day I saw a fairytale Alpine landscape. Green mountains, sturdy chalets hung with flowering baskets, cattle in meadows. But the sight of the gray station wagon, dusty from its long journey of the day before, brought me back to reality. This picturesque village was safe and secure, but soon we would be heading east again, toward Czechoslovakia. Again I felt fear. What if we did not get past the Czech border? What would happen to us if our cargo of Bibles and help was discovered? What if we ended up in prison?

Turning from the window, I decided that there was just time before breakfast to go for a short walk. Taking my Bible I stepped out into the crisp morning. As I walked, taking in the verdant mountain serenity stretching out before me, I reminded the Lord of my dilemma. I told Him that I wanted to help His suffering Church and was not entirely without faith. I knew that our cargo was His responsibility and what He had done before in taking it across borders, He could do again. "But will You do so," I asked Him, "if there is fear in my heart? At the moment there's as much fear as faith."

Coming across one of the little benches that seem to be everywhere in Austria, I sat down for a few minutes. How good it would be if God would talk to me in an audible voice and tell me that He was going to give us a safe border crossing. I was glad I had brought my Bible and thought of the thousands of Czechs who did not have even a portion of Scripture of their own. Opening it, I turned to Psalm 34, written at a time when King David had known fear. The fourth verse stood out for me particularly: "I sought the Lord, and he answered me; he delivered me from all my fears."

I measured those words against my own past life, remembering how afraid I had been formerly to lay my life in God's hands. One fear had been that He would lead me out of England. And indeed, after my surrender to His will, He had done that. But now I knew I'd have been much the poorer if He had allowed me to sit quietly and safely at home. How many adventures He had given me! He had taken me to Africa, then to The Netherlands, and now I was in central Europe. He had not let me down. The verse took on special meaning for me as I made a quick review of the past.

And then verse seven jumped off the page at me: "The angel of the Lord encamps around those who fear him, and he delivers them." Somehow I knew that the Lord was giving me a special assurance through that verse. He was telling me that His angels were with us and I believed that I should take the words *he delivers them* literally as far as our valuable cargo was concerned.

I could not say that my heart was totally free of fear, but there was certainly an increase in faith as my traveling companions and I pulled out of the enchanted village at mid-morning and made for the main road to Vienna. It helped to be moving again. The element of no-turning-back was reinforced as the mileage gauge moved on relentlessly.

The landscape had lost its majestic beauty and a soft rain was falling long before we passed by Vienna onto the relatively short and quiet stretch of highway leading into Czechoslovakia. Little traffic was coming from the direction of the border and just a few cars were going our way. Some bore Dutch license plates. They must be supporters of Ajax Amsterdam, I decided. I felt around in my purse for the ticket to the big soccer game in Trnava the next day. Perhaps the customs official would need it as proof that we really intended to support our Dutch team.

A few miles before the border the two cars stopped and we all got together to pray for the crossing. We used a prayer that we had heard Brother Andrew pray many times: "Lord Jesus, when You were on earth You made blind eyes to see. Will You do the opposite now? We have Bibles and help for Your children beyond this border and the customs officials must not see them. Will You please make seeing eyes blind?" Then we were on our way again. Our goal was almost within view.

It was late afternoon. The rain had stopped, the road was wet as we pulled past the Austrian customs officer into a short stretch of "no man's land" separating Austria and Czechoslovakia. Now very near the Czech border, we could see control towers and barbed wire on top of fences. We pulled up behind a line of six waiting vehicles. Soon I would have my first glimpse behind the mysterious Iron Curtain.

To my left, cars leaving Czechoslovakia were being checked by unsmiling officials dressed in navy blue uniforms with peaked caps. One of them was a slender young man, taller than his colleagues and with a manner less brusque. He looked a little unsure of himself. I wondered if he was new at the job.

My attention turned to the car in front. It was a Volkswagen "bug" bearing a German license plate. To my dismay I watched a particularly officious, portly Czech customs official subject the vehicle to a very thorough search, speaking in clipped German as he did so.

First the occupants had to get out and remove all their luggage from the seats and trunk of the car. The gruff official walked 'round the vehicle, surveyed it, then began to knock on all the panels. Next he went through the inside of the car very carefully. A search even half that thorough would easily reveal our precious Bibles. And then I brought to mind the verse that had helped me in the fairytale village that morning: "The angel of the Lord encamps around those who fear him, and he delivers them."

The "fear" of the Lord was the only fear allowed in my heart, and indeed I noticed with amazement that now that we had actually arrived at the border, there remained no fear of man in my heart. Certainly tension, but not fear.

The surly customs official finished his inspection of the Austrian car and waved the occupants impatiently through. He started to walk toward our car. I held my breath. And then something unusual happened. As if he suddenly remembered that he had other business to attend to, he stopped in his tracks and motioned to the rather hesitant young man I had seen dealing with cars leaving the country. Saying a few words to him in Czech the senior official left and his young colleague advanced toward our car. I started to breathe again. Requesting our passports, he checked them and asked us to open the trunk. This we did and he took a cursory look inside, disturbing none of our luggage. Hitting the roof of the car with the flat of his hand he told us to proceed and we moved slowly into Czechoslovakia.

As soon as we were out of earshot of the border the four of us began to shout our joy that God had brought us this far in safety. Ahead we could also see the other team car and knew that they would be praising God too.

Suddenly weary, I settled into the back seat of the car and closed my eyes. It had been an amazing day. I began to see that faith is an active thing. This morning in that serene Austrian village, the Lord had encouraged me but He had not crossed the border *for* me. I had to do it and when I did, He had honored my small amount of faith. It was as if He was telling me that the very nature of faith is that it has to be tested. And having gone through the test I now noticed something else. I felt stronger as I anticipated the next test.

Knowing that it would soon be dark, we made our way

toward a small town where we were to spend the night. Leen, who was in charge of our teams, had names and addresses of the Christians we were to visit but in order not to be too obvious we were not driving in convoy.

My first impression of Czechoslovakia was that there was an immediate decline in the standard of the road surface compared to that of western Europe. We had to negotiate narrow and often badly paved roads and direction signs were few. When we passed through villages we saw very few people and those we did see all seemed to be dressed in navy blue. There was hardly a child anywhere. Everything seemed muted. The expressions of the few people we saw were passive and unexcited. There was little that spoke of prosperity or progress such as building projects of any size. Along the sides of the road, at regular intervals, were huge signs bearing foreign words we could not decipher. From the presence of lots of red paint and the hammer and sickle, however, we guessed that the local people were being encouraged to put their trust in Communism.

But it was not what we could see that had the greatest effect on me. It was the spirit of the country. From the beginning I sensed a deep oppression. It seemed to hang in the atmosphere. The other three women in our station wagon also experienced this suffocating heaviness. I began to feel even more concerned for the Slovak Christians. Whatever would it be like to live under this oppression all the time?

Spending the night in the small town, we met up the next day with the rest of our team and traveled on to Trnava where the match would be played. Thousands of Slovaks, all dressed in navy blue, jammed the stadium and as the game began I at last saw a display of emotion as people cheered on their team with as much energy as I had ever seen in western Europe. While the Dutch spurred on their Ajax Amsterdam I cheered with the Slovaks and was nearly as disappointed as they were when their team lost.

Later that day we drove to the home of a middle-aged Christian couple who welcomed us with much love. I could not tell that from what they said because they were communicating in German but I could tell it from the smiles and the welcoming kisses of the wife who set before us of some of the most delicious food I had ever tasted. Before Communism took over the country, Czechoslovakia was second, in the opinion of many, to France in cuisine. The home was small and simply furnished, but very neat and clean.

While the wife busied herself in the welcoming of her foreign guests, the husband helped other team members as they unpacked the contents of our cars in the high-walled yard. Some of the many Bibles and books were carried into a shed, and others were taken to a bedroom. I realized that this Christian home was a central point from which a chain of Bibles and books would spread through the country. As the literature was unpacked there were exclamations of delight as the couple saw the new treasures. Of particular interest was a small book with a Czech title bearing the name of the writer, Corrie ten Boom. They obviously recognized the name. So Tante Corrie's message of God's love and the need to forgive our enemies had reached even into Czechoslovakia!

Traveling on, our cars and hearts much lighter now that the help we had brought had been safely transferred, we crossed into the portion of the country known as Bohemia. I loved at once the quiet beauty of the country. This part of Czechoslovakia was more heavily populated and there was an even more pronounced spirit of dejection among the people. There was a droop to their shoulders as if they were carrying a heavy burden and I began to feel very indignant on their behalf. Just one year before they had been rejoicing in the relaxing of strict measures—the Prague Spring, they called it—and then, just eight months ago, the Soviet Union had invaded and put an end to the newly found freedom. I was certain the Christians here felt resentful. How did they deal with it?

I soon had at least a partial answer to my question. Two days later we were invited to a Sunday morning service in a church in a rural area near the Polish border. The speaker was a leading member of the Russian underground Church, a strong, well-built man who addressed the congregation in Russian. A translator turned the Russian into Czech, from Czech it was turned into German for the benefit of our group; but I, not understanding German, was at a disadvantage. I had to wait until somebody in our group had understood a sufficient amount to put it into English. The Russian had gone a long way into his sermon before the sense of it filtered through to me, three languages later.

Suddenly the Russian speaker's voice broke and he began to weep. Trying to control himself he continued with his message. The Czech translator began to weep also, and so did many in the congregation. What on earth was happening? When would a translation finally reach me? Then I heard the Russian speaker phrase a sentence that, judging by the inflection of his voice, seemed to be a question. From the congregation came what seemed to be an affirmative answer, but it was accompanied by much weeping. Finally, the English translation reached me: "The Russian brother has confessed the wrongdoing of the Soviet nation in invading Czechoslovakia and on behalf of the Russian Church he is asking forgiveness of the Czech Christians."

After the sermon was over the Czech Christians crowded 'round their Russian brother and I could tell by the hugs, handshakes, and tears that they were accepting his confession and expressing their forgiveness.

I felt humbled by this incident. I had just been given a glimpse into a very private matter. Soon I would be leaving the country and heading for the free West once again. The Czech Christians would have to live with oppression daily. But I had also been given a glimpse into what makes the suffering Church strong. In their material poverty they were dealing with issues that were truly important. They were obeying Christ. They were growing in Him.

I left Czechoslovakia a different person from the one who entered it. It was as if the Lord had knit my heart with my brothers and sisters in the East. I felt more complete as a Christian for having met them. As the car headed for Holland I was filled with a much deeper desire to do my part to let their story be known in the free West. How could I do it? And then I was amazed at the desire and knew that it was the Lord's work. I, who had always been so concerned for my own safety and well-being, had been led along by the Lord to the place where the needs of others were beginning to be important.

Chapter Six

The School of Prayer

The arrival of the new decade, the 1970s, saw a continuing increase in the requests for help from Christians in East European countries. At the same time, *God's Smuggler* was being published in many languages and confronting more and more Christians in the West with their responsibility to help the suffering Church. This resulted in increased financial giving, in much more prayer, and in the volunteering of many Christians, particularly Americans, to take Bibles and aid to the East. Extra vehicles suitable for carrying help and many more full-time co-workers were added to our little Dutch base in Harderwijk.

The question was often put to Brother Andrew, "Will the fact that you have published a book about your work not alert the East European border guards to what you are doing? Will you not be damaging your ministry?" I had to admit that the question often lurked in the back of my mind, too.

Brother Andrew's consistent reply was, "No, this will not damage the ministry. The Lord is asking us to increase our faith. He has all the power in heaven and on earth and will continue to allow us to cross the borders."

And God did. I began to learn, as I gradually gained understanding and fluency in the Dutch language, that the faith of Brother Andrew and his team was directly related to prayer. It was of enormous importance to the ministry. Each team member who was not traveling met at the office each working day for prayer before work began, and on Monday evenings a large prayer meeting was held, including the husbands and wives of the full-time team members.

It was at these meetings that I began to learn about what Brother Andrew called "spiritual warfare." He taught us that it was right to pray *for* many things, but that we also had to learn to pray *against* things, including Satan's grip on the Communist world with its resulting darkness and oppression. I recalled the suffocating atmosphere of Eastern Europe and my resolve to do what I could to make the story of the suffering Church known in the free West. I could see that a large part of the fulfilling of that desire would lie in a willingness on my part to pray. That would take not only time. It would also take a boldness in praying against the works of Satan. Each involved a new surrendering of rights—my right to my own time use, and, uncomfortably, my "right" to be shy. Now I had to take aggressive authority in Jesus' name. I could not, I discovered, hide behind a natural shyness and enter effectively into spiritual warfare.

But in supporting the suffering Church a much older battle with my rights soon emerged, too. Now and then I crossed the English Channel back to my home in Hastings, East Sussex, and found my family eager to hear all about my adventures. One particular trip, in 1970, occurred at a time when my sister, Sylvia, having gained her biology degree from the University of Sussex, was preparing to do further study at the University of London and was home for a few days. I took the opportunity one Friday to give her detailed accounts of the situation in Eastern Europe, gleaned from the stories of recently returned teams. She listened with intense interest, and then said:

"Why don't we go along to the young people's meeting at church tonight? You could tell what you have learned from being in Holland."

"No," I protested, remembering my childhood fears. "I am very bad at speaking in public. My voice is so soft that nobody would hear me, and the very thought of standing up in front of everybody is terrifying. Don't let's go."

What I was doing, of course, was to stay safely within a known way. It had always frightened me to speak in public and I had worked out a safe lifestyle that left me in control of this fear by simply refusing if at all possible to do so. I had a right to say no, after all; and say no I did.

Sylvia did not press me further and I tried to put the matter out of my mind. I did not succeed. I remembered my thoughts on returning from Czechoslovakia the previous spring. The Christians in that country had impressed me deeply. I had resolved to do all that I could on their behalf. Since then I had learned that for the work to succeed there needed to be prayer. Now I was being offered a small opportunity to inform some English Christians about the suffering Church so that they could pray. But I was unwilling to take it.

And then, very strongly, I remembered Ashburnham, the beautiful conference center where, five years before, I had committed my life to Jesus Christ in a moonlit dormitory room. The words of my prayer of that night echoed in my mind: "I now give up my right to my own will . . . I want to do Your will and be used by You. If You want me to work in a foreign country, I will. If You want me to speak in public, although it seems quite impossible, I will. . . ."

That surrender of my will had resulted in something I had thought I did not want—leaving England. I thought that to leave England meant losing the joy and security of home. But instead of losing anything, I had gained a great deal. Within me was a deep satisfaction over the work I had done in Africa and even more was doing today in The Netherlands. Now I was being confronted with laying down my will again. Could it be that the Lord was asking me to speak a few words to the young people?

"Let's see if we would be welcome," I said at last to Sylvia. "We are well ahead of the average age of the youth group."

If I had been hoping for an obstacle I was to be disappointed, for the youth minister, on receiving my phone call, gave us a hearty welcome. "How are things in Holland?" he said. "Could you tell us about Brother Andrew's work in Eastern Europe?"

"All right," I said, as much to the Lord as to him. "I will try."

That evening Sylvia and I took the bus to the youth group's meeting place not far from the seafront church of my childhood. Our journey took us once again under the shadow of the Norman castle and along the road next to the English Channel. I could not help thinking of a similar journey she and I had made five years previously when I had been so reluctant to accompany her to the retreat. I had looked at the Channel then and compared its gray and rough waves to the restlessness in my heart. How different life was now! The Channel was equally choppy this evening, but now I had a fulfilled heart.

Even so, as we walked into the meeting place I anticipated the evening with trepidation. Could I talk about the suffering Church to these young people in a way that would help them identify with its heartbeat? I felt my own heartbeat quicken and my mouth become dry. While the young people sang I desperately hoped I would be able to follow my notes. "Lord," I prayed, "please send Your Holy Spirit to help me tell this true story well. I cannot do it without Your help."

Too soon the songs were ended, and all eyes were on me. As I made my way to the front, I could feel my legs trembling and remembered days in junior school when I knew the answer to a question but refused to give it because that meant speaking out in front of others.

As I stood there, everyone waiting, I prayed . . . then began. I wished I could stop the tremor in my voice. "Speak *up*, Pamela!" a childhood teacher's scolding echoed from the past. There was so much to coordinate . . . the volume of my voice, the sequence of my thoughts, and, to my surprise, an interaction with those in front of me. I saw gray eyes, and brown ones, wistful ones, bespectacled ones, confident eyes, shy eyes. But as I stumbled forward an amazing thing began to happen. Instead of seeing a menacing group, I saw individuals. All seemed to be watching me intently and I saw that I should address them not only as a group, but also as separate people.

The starting point of my talk had to be the great change in my life that came about when I submitted myself to God's will in this same youth group. Then came a brief account of my time in Africa. I was relieved that I had been speaking for about five minutes and had managed to keep going. Again I found myself surprised. The room was quiet and the young people were listening intently. I felt courage rising.

Next came an account of the East European Church. I decided that the best way to make the Christians live would be to talk about certain individuals . . . about Ildiko from Hungary with her pale pink twinset and tired eyes telling how she rose at 5 A.M. to pray for the Christians in China . . . about the Russian brother in northern Czechoslovakia who asked forgiveness of the Czech Christians for his nation's sin in invading their country. I told about the joy I had seen on the faces of those receiving Bibles and help. *O Lord,* I prayed, as I looked into the young people's faces, *help them see that they have a responsibility to the suffering Church. And when they see it, use them to help Your people.*

I decided to end with an example I had heard Brother Andrew use and read from 2 Corinthians 8: "At the present time your plenty will supply what they need, so that in turn their plenty will supply what you need. Then there will be equality. . . ." And I finished with words something like these: "There must be equality in the Body of Christ. With a physical body, one part cannot grow faster than another part without the whole body being put out of joint. And so it is with the Body of Christ. We in the West cannot expect to grow faster than our suffering brothers and sisters in the East. Let us ask the Lord how we can do our part in bringing equality, whether it is by giving, or praying, or going."

I resumed my place at the back of the room, glad to be sitting down, and breathed a prayer of thanks to the Lord for getting me through the little talk. They listened, I told myself, and not just halfheartedly. They were keen to hear every word. When the meeting ended the young people crowded 'round with questions and it was ten o'clock before Sylvia and I could make our way home again.

I did a lot of thinking on the way back to our little red brick house. This evening had been a testing. I had always said I could not speak in public. Now, with the Lord's help, I had. Not only had I gotten through it, but people had actually been interested. And there was something more. Within myself was a deep satisfaction. I had to admit that I had actually enjoyed it. The longing I had had to make the needs of the suffering Church known in the West had been partly fulfilled in that little meeting.

God had known all along that it would be that way once I relinquished my will to His on the issue. I found myself remembering the song once again, the one He had used on the night of my first surrender, and the one I had recalled on returning from my first overseas adventure in Africa:

> *Praise to the Lord, who o'er all things so wondrously*
>   *reigneth,*
> *Shelters thee under his wings, yea, so gently sustaineth!*
> *Hast thou not seen how thy desires e'er have been granted*
>   *in what he ordaineth?*

I was glad to get back to Holland. I did not want to miss any of the developments in the ministry and there were plenty of those. We did not have enough staff, vehicles, and Bibles to meet the requests for help that continued to pour in from Eastern Europe. Soon there were plans to expand our headquarters to include a depot with much more room for staff and supplies, and before long the plans were realized.

All the co-workers involved in the ministry to Eastern Europe moved their supplies and vehicles to the new depot, and just Brother Andrew, the secretarial staff, and I remained in the old headquarters building in Harderwijk. Although much of his heart was still in Eastern Europe, Brother Andrew was turning his attention increasingly to other areas of the world enclosed by so-called Curtains, whether Iron, Sugar Cane, or the mysterious dark curtain that cuts off the Muslim world.

While there was an opportunity, now and then, to travel to Eastern Europe, my work was mainly in the Harderwijk headquarters and never had I been so busy. As I became more familiar with Dutch, I spent a great deal of time translating the mission's prayer letter into English and sending it to the representatives in English speaking countries throughout the world. There was still a great deal of counseling to be done by mail and thanks to full-time and part-time helpers, I was able to see that each person who contacted us received a personal letter in reply. It was sometimes necessary to work long extra hours in order to keep up with the amount of work.

But there was also time, on weekends, for leisure. One of my favorite activities was to take my bike, usually with a friend, and make for the woods to the east. I loved to breathe the fresh air and take in the beauty of the trees. How quiet it was here, far from the intense work at the office.

One day I noticed a small house in the woods, clean and neat with a well-maintained yard. I found myself again wishing that I had a real home of my own. But it wasn't to be—not for now. I repeated Robert Frost's lines:

> *The woods are lovely, dark and deep,*
> *But I have promises to keep. . . .*

Perhaps the Lord did have a home for me one day, but it was not so now. I had work to do.

I was happy enough with the two small rooms I had inherited from Riska in the little terraced house near the old harbor. I had done a little work on Riska's rooms. The walls I painted white and I'd added green and blue accessories, my favorite color combination. The bed/sitting room was just large enough to hold my bed, a bookcase, a small coffee table, and two small wicker chairs. A large black oil stove in the corner kept me warm in the winter. My kitchen contained a stove top, a sink, table, and refrigerator all of diminutive proportion.

It was good to have my own little domain and I spent much time there alone. But I did not need to be lonely. Miss de Graaf, my elderly, white-haired landlady, who had greeted me with a flood of Dutch on my first day in Holland, had gradually, as I learned her language, become a source of much help and information to me. And nowhere had I drunk such delicious coffee as in her sitting room downstairs.

And there were also lots of opportunities to make new friends and to explore The Netherlands, including the ancient city of Harderwijk in which I lived. As I explored I learned that the town received its charter in the thirteenth century, and found many places of historical interest, some of them hidden behind the twentieth-century bustle of the old fishing town. One fact of great interest to me was that in the days before Harderwijk's university was destroyed by fire, Linnaeus, the famous Swedish botanist, after whose method plant life is named, studied in this city. Plants and their names had fascinated me ever since my years with the Hastings Parks and Gardens Department at home in southern England.

Further afield I spent hours in art museums and also discovered an old castle where the guide incorporated into his tour an explanation of the background of Dutch sayings and colloquial expressions. This insight into their language helped me to understand the people and culture better. Because of the nature of our work it was best not to give it too much publicity in Harderwijk. I therefore did not have too many friends outside the work circle. On Sundays I joined my landlady and most of my colleagues at a small, independent fellowship called The Full Gospel Church. Its members were very supportive of the mission work to Eastern Europe.

Now and then, when Corrie ten Boom was in Holland, I visited her and Ellen and was able to help in their work from time to time. A project I particularly enjoyed was transcribing the tapes of interviews to be used in the upcoming book about Tante Corrie's life.

Authors John and Elizabeth Sherrill were working hard on the project and once I was given the opportunity to accompany Tante Corrie and Elizabeth on a visit to Vught Concentration Camp where Tante Corrie and her sister Betsie ten Boom were imprisoned before their deportation to Ravensbruck. Elizabeth, whose friends called her "Tibby," was slim and brown-haired and I could see she was a very sensitive and reflective woman. I was impressed by her careful questioning of Tante Corrie. Clearly she was going to do her best to see that every statement in this new book was accurate.

The site of the concentration camp of Vught was in Brabant in the south of Holland, and as we drove there, the normally talkative Corrie ten Boom was rather quiet. I wondered what she was thinking. Was she remembering a time a quarter of a century ago when she and her sister Betsie had been taken to this place in wartime? For their part in helping to save Jewish lives, the Ten Boom family had been arrested, their father had died in prison, and while the rest of the family had been released, Corrie and Betsie had been incarcerated.

On arrival at the site of the concentration camp, the three of us walked along a grassy approach to the gates.

To our right was a row of trees. "They shone lights on us as we walked along here," said Tante Corrie.

"Who did?" asked Tibby.

"The soldiers. They had strong flashlights," replied Tante Corrie. Tibby made notes with a pencil in a small notebook as we walked.

"Where were those soldiers, Corrie?" she then asked. "Were they standing among the trees?"

"I do not remember," said Tante Corrie with a tired sound in her voice. "Whatever does it matter whether they were in the trees or among them?"

I could see that it was distressing to Tibby to require Corrie ten Boom to remember details from a very difficult past. As she tried to explain the importance of small detail, I felt a rising respect for writers. It would surely be necessary, but also very difficult, to present the truth in a way that would grip readers. I wondered how successful she and her husband, John, would be in telling Tante Corrie's story. Would the name *The Hiding Place* ever become a household word among Christians? These repeated contacts with Tante Corrie had a peculiar feel about them, as if in some way I could not yet see they were all of a piece, leading somewhere.

Back at Brother Andrew's headquarters, the months progressed and on all sides the work continued to expand. More and more my life was taken up with providing help for the suffering Church. I could not often travel to the East myself, but my help in the background made it possible for others to go.

Then one day I had a strange little experience that set my mind in an unexpected direction. I was alone in the office since it was necessary to finish a project after hours. The telephone rang and I found myself on the line with one of the faithful part-time travelers to Eastern Europe. I had not talked to him before, but had heard his name in the prayer meetings. He was a member of the American military service, stationed in Holland, and he took advantage of time off to help in Eastern Europe. Having been in Holland for several years I was used to dealing with foreign accents, but this man's voice nearly defeated me. It took me about three attempts before I could decipher his name, although he said it very slowly . . . Peter Highland. The *i* was pronounced like a very long and slow *a*. Finally I wrote down the correct spelling and when the conversation was over passed Pete's message on to the co-worker for whom it was intended.

"Wherever does that man come from?" I asked. "I could hardly understand him."

"Texas," was the reply.

I was curious. Did all Texans have accents like that? If so, going there must be like visiting a foreign country. All the other Americans I had dealt with I could understand quickly. I liked the Americans. Their generous help had had a great deal to do with the expansion of the ministry. Perhaps I would have the opportunity to visit the States one day.

In the summer of 1971 a joyous event took place in our family—the marriage of my sister, Sylvia, to Bruce Baker. Bruce had theological training and hoped to become a pastor. They had met when they were students at the University of Sussex and when Sylvia and Bruce both went to London for further studies and work, their friendship soon proved destined to turn into the most permanent of relationships. I felt honored when Sylvia asked me to be her bridesmaid—she planned to have just one—and I gladly complied. The marriage took place in our old home church on the seafront on a sunny July day. Sylvia looked as radiant as I supposed every bride should look and she had much joy in becoming the wife of her tall and handsome Bruce.

After an outdoor reception, the bride and groom left and I had to admit to mixed feelings. My sister had been my closest friend and adviser ever since I had given my life to the Lord. Now another person had come between us. Would we still know the same closeness?

But there was another reason for the mixed feelings. I had so longed for a home of my own and here was my younger sister getting married before I did. The wedding served to remind me that I'd made the surrender of my will with my mind but that I had to keep working to surrender my heart as well. As I traveled back to Holland I felt a strange new loneliness. It had been so good to see all the family together, including my brother, Digger, and his wife. He worked for the Civil Service and had a little daughter. But again I found myself thinking—Digger was married, Sylvia was married, and I, although the oldest, was the only one left single. I had to admit that one of the reasons why I gave myself so intently to the work in Holland was to shut out the longing I often felt for a husband and children. But on the other hand, the fact that I did not have them enabled me to do much more for the suffering Church. While I knew that God had not made a mistake, now that I was in my late twenties the desire not to be alone for the rest of my life was a strong one. During the hours by myself in my little white room with its green and blue cushions in the wicker chairs, I often prayed that one day God would give me a husband and children and a home of my own.

Then one day shortly after my return from Sylvia's wedding, I had a new kind of experience with laying down my rights. That morning a particularly bright sun reflected off the white walls through the large picture window. As

I prayed it was as though the Lord spoke to my heart, saying something like this: *You have prayed much for a husband and children. I want you now to lay down that prayer and commit it to Me fully.*

I believed the Lord was telling me that He wanted me to stop praying for a husband. I did. I had a new assurance that whether the answer was yes or no, He had heard me and the result was safe in His hands. "Then, Lord," I prayed, "please use me to be a blessing to the children of others."

Shortly after this, while visiting friends in London, I attended a small reception. While I was introduced to a couple I had never met before, it was again as if the Lord spoke to me inside: *This couple does not have children and they long for a family. Pray for them.* Back in Holland I did not forget the couple and remembered them in my times of prayer. About a year later I heard about them again—they had just become the parents of a beautiful child called Josephine. I felt a joy in my heart that I believed in some ways equaled that of Josephine's parents. The joy was partly a sharing in their happiness, but it was much more. It was the knowledge that in some mysterious way, God was taking my own loneliness and using it to help others in a manner that would not have been possible had I been married.

I began to see that when people lay down their lives for the Lord Jesus, He leads them along paths on which they have to prove that they meant it. As the years progressed, co-workers came and went. Most were married with families. When tempted to envy the coziness and lack of loneliness of their homes I employed a help that never failed. I quoted a verse from the Bible to myself. Time and again it put things in perspective. It had struck me with particular force during my Bible reading one day. Psalm 84:11:

"No good thing does he withhold from those whose walk is blameless." I thought long and hard about that verse. It told me that God does not keep any good thing from those who obey Him. I believed I was obeying Him. Therefore, at any point in my life, He was giving me what was best for me at that particular time. Marriage was in itself a good thing. But it was obviously not the best thing for me at the moment, otherwise God would have given it.

That was what this verse promised. Therefore, I needed to conclude that my single state was not only good, but was the very best thing for me in God's loving plan. It was better for me than marriage. The truth behind this verse was the strongest sustaining factor in my being enabled to live a single life in a victorious way.

After I had been with Brother Andrew for about three years, my co-worker, Riska, who had been such a help to me from the beginning, left to be part of a missionary endeavor in Nepal. By now the English division of our work had the help of several full- and part-time assistants. And the Dutch depot continued to expand. There was simply too much work for us to handle. At our Monday night prayer meetings we prayed that God would give us the right new co-workers to help take care of the volume of work.

That prayer was answered partly by the provision of new assistance in the United States. Bill Butler and his wife, Bettie, based in California, agreed to take over the representation of the Dutch work in America.

In the summer of 1972, Brother Andrew asked me to visit the United States to get to know Bill and Bettie and to help them and their staff become familiar with the work in Holland. For the best part of two weeks I stayed in Santa Ana, California, and although I did some work in trying to inform the new American co-workers of the Dutch ministry, it seemed to me that they were doing all they could to give their English visitor the best time possible. There were trips to the Pacific, to the mountains, Disneyland, and many other places, and I left with my feeling reinforced that the Americans were among the kindest and most generous people in the world.

But I also left with the impression that I probably would not want to live in their country. Life moved too fast, and there was so much smog, near Los Angeles anyway!

Through the years my visits to England continued, but now I visited London, and Sylvia's family, as often as I returned to the family home on the south coast. Sylvia and Bruce had become the parents of two beautiful children, Gideon and Naomi. Their church in London gave me several opportunities to tell about the work in Eastern Europe and I found that God gave me the courage to get up and speak. Although I continued to be nervous, public speaking had lost its terror. People listened and responded. I saw that God used me and this fulfilled me deeply.

And then quite unexpectedly a change came into my life. In 1975 the work in Holland had grown to such proportions that we did not know how best to plan for expansion. Brother Andrew accepted the offer of management consultants in the United States to come to Holland and make an analysis of the ministry. Over a period of several months, a thorough analysis was made and a far-reaching reorganization was suggested.

After much prayer, Brother Andrew decided to act upon the advice and I backed him in his decision. But the reorganization left me in a strange position. Much of the work that I had done would now be taken over and developed in different departments. It would mean a great relief in the workload for me, but somehow I had the feeling that

I no longer belonged. Did I still have a place here? Or was my work in Holland coming to a close?

At first I did not couple these events with another piece of news. One day early in 1976 somebody said to me, "Have you heard that Tante Corrie's companion is going to be married soon? They are looking for somebody to take her place. How about you?" I assumed that the suggestion was a lighthearted one. Ellen de Kroon was a registered nurse. Corrie ten Boom was now nearly 84 years old with a heart that was not strong. Apart from that, I was just not the type to be a companion. I dismissed the suggestion.

Shortly afterward, however, I had to recall it again. On my desk at work I found a note from Brother Andrew. He too had heard of Ellen's decision and wondered if I'd like to take a three-month break from the work in Holland in order to help Corrie ten Boom. He said that it would be a very good experience for me to have a long break after more than seven years of work in Holland. I decided to dismiss that suggestion too. Even for three months I was not the companion type.

But in the following days, I felt a tug in my conscience. There had now been two suggestions that I help Corrie ten Boom and I had not given them serious consideration. What if the Lord were speaking to me and I was not listening?

There was one way to find out. I decided that on the following Sunday I would spend time in my little apartment in prayer. I knew that the week was going to be so busy that I would have to wait until Sunday for an opportunity to be alone for any length of time.

So it was that on the afternoon of February 29, 1976, I went to my square dining room table and with my Bible before me, propped my elbows on the table and cupped my face in my hands. I needed to make another surrender to the Lord. Perhaps I was being asked to leave the work of Brother Andrew. Deliberately, slowly, painfully then, I relinquished everything that I loved about Holland—my work, the language, my friends, the contact with the suffering Church, the exciting, refreshing, fast-moving nature of the ministry—and I told the Lord that I was available if He wanted to move me out of it, even if it was His plan that I spend a little while helping Corrie ten Boom. After my prayer I felt a new lightheartedness but had no idea what step to take next. The road ahead still had no shape.

My thoughts were interrupted by a knock on the door and upon opening it I discovered Celia, a tall red-headed member of our team who worked with me on English correspondence. Celia said she knew I had been feeling uncertain about my future and wanted to pray for me. I quickly agreed and told Celia that I had just laid before the Lord any hold I might have on the work in Holland.

After we had prayed together for a moment, Celia began telling me about a picture that had just come into her mind. It was as though she were telling me something that I would see in the future.

"Pam," she said, "I see you on a very fast journey. The road is flashing past very quickly and so are trees and houses and fields. You are traveling to many different places. And the Lord is saying to you, 'Do not be afraid. I will be with you.'"

The usually funny and talkative Celia was serious and quiet and obviously deeply impressed by the picture she had seen. She repeated it to me at my request, and after we had drunk a cup of tea together, she left my little home.

It seemed I had just closed the door behind her when the telephone rang. It was the first time that it had rung that day.

"Hello, Pam," said a friendly voice. "This is Ellen." I was surprised that so soon after my prayer of relinquishment I should be confronted with Tante Corrie's helper, but I was glad to hear from her and asked what I could do for her.

"We are wondering if you could help correct some English copy for the printer," said Ellen in reply.

Somehow I felt there must be more to her phone call than a desire for correct English copy.

"Why are you really calling me, Ellen?" I asked, surprised at my boldness.

There was a very short pause at the end of the line. "Well," she said, "I do not want to run ahead of the Lord, but this afternoon when she was praying Tante Corrie felt very strongly that you are the one she should ask to help her when I leave to be married."

Telling Ellen that I would call her back shortly, I sat once again at my dining room table with my head cupped in my hands. What an interesting series of events had taken place this afternoon. First I had surrendered my rights to my own future anew to the Lord. Then Celia had arrived and had seen a fast-moving picture that appeared to apply to me. And now Ellen de Kroon had called to say that this afternoon—probably just at the time when I was laying down my rights before the Lord—Tante Corrie had received the assurance that it was right to ask me to join her.

Curious, I said to myself, thinking back to the day I'd come to Holland to help Brother Andrew on a temporary basis. That was seven years ago! Now, I picked up the phone and called Ellen to say I was willing to meet Tante Corrie again very soon. "Maybe there's something I can do to help. Just for a few weeks, of course, until you find someone more suitable. . . ."

Chapter Seven

The Work Comes First

On a windy March morning a short time afterward, I rang the doorbell of a semi-detached house on a busy boulevard in a suburb of Haarlem called Overveen. This was Corrie ten Boom's new home, the first that belonged to her since she had sold the family watchshop and embarked on her world travels. I was wearing a belted tweed winter coat and had the collar turned up against the penetrating wind. Since living in ever-windy Holland I had been glad for my thick head of hair, which I had allowed to grow to shoulder length. It helped keep me warm.

Once again, following the Dutch custom of taking flowers to the hostess when on a visit of any length, I was clutching a bunch of yellow tulips in my left hand. Many had been the time in the last seven years when I had stood on Tante Corrie's doorstep but never had I felt the mounting hesitation I now felt as I waited for Ellen to answer my ring. I hoped that in the time between Ellen's phone call last Sunday and this morning, Tante Corrie would have thought better of asking me to become her temporary companion.

Soon Ellen opened the front door and ushered me in-

BIRDVILLE
BAPTIST CHURCH
LIBRARY

side. Taking my coat she greeted me with the news that Tante Corrie was having a day in bed. Her doctor had suggested that at her age and with her heart condition this would be a good idea. This frightened me anew. Wouldn't Corrie ten Boom almost *have* to have a companion with nurses' training? Ellen invited me to go upstairs to Tante Corrie's bedroom at the back of the first floor. She was expecting me and looking forward to my coming, Ellen assured me, probably sensing how I was feeling.

During the past seven years Tante Corrie had never lost that aura of true purity that had impressed me at our first meeting. It was with a soft tread and a reverence that I mounted the steep staircase. It was certainly a good idea that at 83 years of age she was taking a day of rest. I would probably find her reclining in a darkened room.

On the first floor landing I knocked softly on the left-hand door of the two facing me. "Come in," said a clear alto voice immediately.

Going 'round the door I found myself in a light and airy room full of color and flowers. The walls were decked with pictures and old and new photographs. In one corner was a small organ, in another a desk. There was an easy chair in a central position and over to my left on a very low bed lay Tante Corrie. She was resting against a mound of pillows, wearing short-sleeved yellow pajamas with brown and gold embroidery on the lapels. Her silver hair was not arranged in the familiar roll around her head but was hanging to her shoulders, giving her a rather vulnerable appearance. Her light-colored blanket was almost completely covered with books and papers. The usual blue and discerning eyes behind gold-rimmed spectacles met mine. "*Welkom, kind,*" she said.

Approaching her bed to shake her hand and thank her

for her welcome, I smiled to myself that she had used the Dutch word for *child* in her greeting. I was in my early thirties, hardly a child, but being more than half a century her junior I probably seemed like one to her. Placing the yellow tulips beside her, I took a closer look at the amazing array of papers and books on her bed. Letters, sheets of manuscript, concordances, Bibles, dictionaries. This may be a day in bed and perhaps it was good for her heart, but this elderly lady was certainly not resting her mind.

Laying down a sheaf of papers, Tante Corrie turned all her attention to me after thanking me for the flowers and inviting me to pull the easy chair closer to her bed.

"Well, child," she said, looking at me with intent interest. "What has the Lord told you?"

For a brief moment I wanted to tell her the whole story . . . how I felt that my time with Brother Andrew was drawing to a close, how somebody had suggested I offer to help her, how I had dismissed the suggestion, how I had again surrendered to the Lord my right to my own future. And how He had ordered a series of events that indicated it may be right for me to offer to help her for a little while. But I was already being influenced by Tante Corrie's personality. She was so direct and to the point! I decided to keep my answer short.

"Well, Tante Corrie," I began slowly, "I am willing to help you. . . ."

"Praise the Lord," she said. "That is settled then!" And for her the matter seemed to be.

But, I protested to myself, *I did not really finish the sentence.* I meant to say I'd be willing to help for a few months until she found somebody who was a true companion type and, more importantly, a nurse.

Tante Corrie, however, had already embarked on a description of her next journey to the United States. She told me that during the past few years her ministry had been mainly in America where she had a great many opportunities to speak. She was to travel by way of Geneva, where she was to work on a book with one of her nephews, then to New York to meet representatives of Fleming H. Revell, her publisher, then to Miami for an Easter sunrise service at which she was to be the main speaker. American Christians apparently rose before dawn to commemorate the resurrection of the Lord Jesus. That was a nice custom but were they not perhaps asking a bit much of an old lady to expect her to rise before dawn too?

Tante Corrie had no such question mark. She went on. Later in April, Gordon College in Wenham, Massachusetts, was to present her with an honorary doctorate. The idea surprised me. Why would she be interested in a doctorate she had not earned? Would she be called Dr. ten Boom henceforth? I did not question her about it.

There was a kind of mirth in her eyes as Tante Corrie explained that her itinerary in America would include seventeen cities. I could hardly believe my ears. Surely at nearly eighty-four this was simply too much? I had the sudden feeling that she knew that I had regarded her as very elderly and delicate and that she was looking forward to proving me wrong.

Next I heard Tante Corrie say something that caused me to swallow hard. Looking at me kindly, but firmly, she said: "You must know, child, that you will always have second place. The work comes first."

There was a pensiveness in her voice. What situation was she visualizing, I wondered? I could not imagine what she meant, but felt sure that I was going to be in for some uncomfortable moments if the work really did come first every time. What would I have thought if I had been able to foresee events lying in the future? But for now I tried to cheer myself with the thought that I had better take one step at a time.

I went back to Harderwijk to make my temporary farewells to Brother Andrew and the staff. "It won't be for long," I said. And to underscore this I made arrangements for a co-worker to take up only temporary residence in my apartment. I packed two suitcases with clothes of varying weights which I hoped would be suitable for climates all over America and presented myself at the appointed time on Tante Corrie's doorstep.

During my week at Tante Corrie's house before we were to fly out, I was glad to have my own little bedroom under the eaves on the third floor. It was a relief to retreat to it as often as I could, for the household was extremely busy and at times hard to handle even with Ellen's help. The telephone rang often, there were visitors, meals to cook, plans to make, suitcases to pack. Busy as I was in my work for Brother Andrew, I also had a great deal of freedom. I had my own large office and at the end of the day there was the solitude of my own apartment. Here, in Tante Corrie's household, things were quite different. I could see that she was expecting me to stand with her in all aspects of the work. And the day was not over at 5:30 P.M. but continued into the evening. What a relief to close the door to my little bedroom late at night. I hoped that in our travels I would often have my own room.

Ellen did her best to give me some basic training during that week before we left for America. She provided me with a list of foods Tante Corrie liked, explained how and why she took certain medications, and told me the kind of thing to expect on our travels. "People recognize Tante Corrie," she said. "She appears in the final segment of the movie 'The Hiding Place' and she's often on television.

She likes to take the opportunity to talk to as many people as possible."

My mind went back to the time six years earlier when John and Elizabeth Sherrill were working on the book of that title and I had wondered if the name *The Hiding Place* would ever become a household word among Christians. It had. Not only had the book become a bestseller, but the film had also become widely known. I had seen it at its Dutch premiere the previous year and had wept at its message. Somehow the director had managed to convey Corrie ten Boom's life message in a skillful fashion so that I, and presumably tens of thousands of others, had been left with a strong impression, as Corrie had so often put it, that God's love is much stronger than the deepest darkness. Even the darkness of the murder of her closest relatives and confinement in a concentration camp.

During that week of preparation in Haarlem, I began to learn something that was basic to Corrie ten Boom's personality. She was disarmingly—perhaps even alarmingly —honest and had no fear of expressing her opinion. While I could see that this made for a good working relationship I was not sure that I could be equally frank. I had always regarded myself as a private person and did not relish the thought of sharing my deepest thoughts with anybody else.

The unusual thing about Tante Corrie's directness, however, was that it was often balanced by an endearing sensitivity. One morning, after having received several coiffure lessons from Ellen, I was concentrating on wrapping Tante Corrie's fine silvery hair around her hair roll and securing it with pins. As usual I was all thumbs and wished once again that I were a more practical person. In the end I decided that I had done as presentable a job as I could manage and stood back. Tante Corrie did not even

cast a glance in the mirror but said, "Thank you, child."
She had apparently sensed my uncertainty and her lack of
concern about what the mirror might reveal endeared me
to her.

But then, I found her looking at my own thick head of
hair. "Why don't you think about a short hairstyle?" she
asked. "It will take a lot of time to deal with long hair
when we are traveling."

I felt slightly indignant. Surely the way I wore my hair
was purely my own matter? I liked wearing my hair shoulder length.

"No, Tante Corrie, I want to keep it this way," I said
firmly.

"All right, child," she said, making for her desk to deal
with the morning's correspondence. Her words during
our interview came into my mind: "You will always have
second place. The work comes first." Was this a little test
of what it meant to be "second" to the work? For the sake
of that work, would I have to change my hairstyle?

During the next few days I enjoyed the warm, open,
cozy nature of Tante Corrie's home. She and Ellen were
careful to communicate anything of importance. If there
was a telephone call, the essence of the call was carefully
passed on. Backgrounds to letters were explained.

This must be part of harmonious living together. For
more than seven years with Brother Andrew's office I had
been alone and to a large extent my thoughts and decisions were my own. I'd come to think of that privacy as a
need to be carefully guarded. Now, for the next few
months, I would have to learn to share everything with
another person.

One afternoon I was delighted to see in the mail an
envelope addressed to me in Sylvia's familiar writing. As
soon as possible I would retreat to my room to read her

news, and to see what advice she might have for me now. Although we led very different lives, and had been separated for most of the last ten years, we were still very close, corresponded often, and I regarded her as my main mentor.

My plan to read Sylvia's letter in private, however, was soon aborted. Tante Corrie saw me remove the letter from the pile and asked who had sent it. On hearing that it was my sister, Tante Corrie suggested that we read it right then.

I hesitated at this invasion of privacy. Yet I did not want to appear rude, so I slowly slit the envelope and extracted the pages telling myself that Tante Corrie didn't know the background to any of Sylvia's remarks and would lose interest in the letter before long.

The opposite was the case. Tante Corrie listened to my reading of Sylvia's long epistle with much interest. When there were parts that she did not understand, she asked questions and I found myself quite eagerly telling her about Sylvia and Bruce and little Gideon and Naomi, about Bruce's hopes to become a pastor soon, and about Sylvia's important role in my coming to know and serve the Lord.

When I had finished telling, I felt my respect for Tante Corrie rise. She had not simply wanted to know the contents of my letter; she was genuinely interested in all that interested me. And she showed that by praying for Sylvia in our prayer time that night. I began to see that my desire for privacy was something I would need to surrender to the Lord. Life for the next few months would not be private. It would require openness and frankness with another person. She had done her best to make me feel welcome in her world, and I would need to do the same for her.

The week progressed, bags were packed, passports and tickets were readied, and we took leave of Ellen who was staying in Holland to make preparations for her wedding in the summer. On a Thursday evening in early April 1976, Tante Corrie and I were driven to Amsterdam Airport and boarded a plane for Geneva. She missed no chances to tell anyone who would listen about the love of God being stronger than the deepest darkness. She talked to airport personnel and stewardesses and to any passenger who showed an interest in the silver-haired elderly lady in her royal blue coat with silver fur collar. She had instructed me to bring along as many copies of *The Hiding Place* as I could carry so that she could give them away.

Still very much feeling my way in my new job, I began to learn what kinds of things were helpful to Tante Corrie. She liked to begin each day with a cup of tea in bed after which there would be a Bible reading and prayer and planning for the coming hours. I loved planning. It was my practice to make a detailed list of things to be done in any day. Although Tante Corrie had no objection to my way of working, she did not make notes of things needing to be done. I soon realized that this was because she could never count on any definite block of time. People and their needs crowded into her day, taking her time and energy . . . and ruining all hope that I could tick off all the items on my list. I was going to need to learn to give up accomplishing if I wanted to blend my personality with that of my very determined new leader.

Leaving Geneva for New York, Tante Corrie took advantage of the trans-Atlantic crossing to prepare me for working in the United States. It would not be entirely strange to me to be in America because I had had a taste of American life during my visit to California on behalf of Brother Andrew four years earlier. "Americans have a real flair for living," she said, her blue eyes shining. "Germans taught me how to think but Americans have taught me how to live."

"The Americans are very generous people," she said later. "But they also expect a lot of you. I believe you will find grace in their eyes and that they will accept you."

Immediately on arrival in New York, Tante Corrie embarked on a business discussion with representatives of her publisher. I was impressed that even after a long and tiring plane flight she had at her fingertips a list of questions to which she needed answers in connection with forthcoming writing.

After several hours we were on our way again, this time to Miami, where a couple of days later, rising at 3:30 A.M., she was the speaker at the Easter sunrise service at the Marine Stadium. I sat on the platform while she spoke and it seemed to me that I was dreaming. Was I really in Florida at the crack of dawn with the sun rising over the ocean behind me and lighting the faces of an audience of 7,000 people?

Before long we found ourselves near Boston, where Gordon College presented Tante Corrie with the degree "Doctor of Humane Letters." I had been curious why she, who never talked about her accomplishments apart from liking people to know that she was "Holland's first licensed woman watchmaker," would be interested in an honorary degree from an American college. I discovered that the accepting of it had to do with taking yet another opportunity, this time in an academic world, of presenting her message. She was not interested in the degree for its own sake, or in being called "Dr. ten Boom." Her own words after receiving her honor confirmed to me the intent of her heart.

She told of an Indian Christian who, when asked

whether all the honor he received made him proud, answered, "When the donkey trod on the garments that had been laid on the road to Jerusalem, did that make him proud? Of course not, he knew that they were for Jesus and not for him.

"That's how I feel, too," Tante Corrie said. "If you tell me there was something good in my books, in the movie, talks, and deeds, then I want you to know the praise is for Jesus, not me. All the honor is due Him. He was victor, He is victor, and He will be victor. He never gives in and we two will win, Jesus and I—Jesus and Corrie ten Boom, Jesus and the donkey."

Jesus and I. That was obviously the passion of Corrie ten Boom's life and work. There was no room for anything that was not directly related to her ministry.

From the beginning, I loved the United States. There was a freedom to work that I had known nowhere else. And the country was so beautiful and so large. It seemed strange here to be boarding a plane without a passport. I had never done that in Europe. While Tante Corrie settled into the aisle seat with the ease of a seasoned traveler and took a book to read or a notebook in which to write, I usually stared in fascination from the aircraft window. I took in the waterways of the Southeast coast, New York, Boston, Niagara Falls, the plains of the Midwest, the redwood forests of Northern California, hazy Los Angeles, sunny San Diego.

Up and down we went, all over the United States. As the various planes took off and landed, roads flashed by and so did trees, houses, and fields. And in my mind I heard the words of red-headed Celia in my little apartment in Holland: "Pam, I see you on a very fast journey. You are traveling to many different places. And the Lord is saying to you, 'Do not be afraid. I will be with you.' "

I was enjoying this new life. To my own surprise, since I'd thought of myself as so ill-equipped for the job, I wrote in a letter home to my parents: "I am liking this more than anything I have ever done."

I noticed that when Tante Corrie spoke, she kept her messages very simple. They told about her experiences of God's love while she was in the concentration camp, of the necessity of forgiving our enemies, and about how important it was to be ready for the return of the Lord Jesus. Everywhere people flocked to large meetings and they listened. The uncomplicated way in which Tante Corrie spoke touched me and I wanted to learn from it. I saw that she made important points through the use of stories. I reminded myself that whenever I could I must keep a journal of this adventure. Perhaps one day I would have a story to tell as well. In the meantime I was glad that I had had some practice at speaking to audiences for in many cases she asked me to address the people with information about her prayer magazine and books.

Although she loved her work, it was clear that it took a great toll on Tante Corrie. Often her face was drawn with fatigue and she suffered debilitating digestive upsets. But however she felt, the work came first for her. She kept her promises and appointments. While on the one hand I greatly enjoyed my work, on the other hand I was also going through my share of fatigue. The travel was never-ending, and so were the details that had to be arranged. Plane tickets, accommodations, unpacking, ironing, laundry, re-packing, correspondence, interviews. And people, people. Often I longed for some private life, but there was none. At airports, shops, and restaurants she was recognized. I grew tired not just of constant traveling, but of the lack of time of my own.

One day I decided to talk to Tante Corrie about it. "How

is it that you have such love for people?" I asked her. "It is an unconditional kind of love. You accept everybody. I don't. I don't like the way these unknown people barge in on our time and energy."

"Child," she answered, "you and I have got to learn to become mirrors of God's love. A mirror does not do very much. It simply hangs in the right direction."

And on another occasion when I complained mildly about being tired, Tante Corrie asked me, "Is there a sin in your life . . . self-pity, perhaps? Confess it and surrender it."

That was something you could never accuse Tante Corrie of, self-pity. I was beginning to see what she meant by her words at our interview, "You will always have second place. The work comes first." I was going to have to give up my privacy and live as Tante Corrie lived. But that would not happen overnight. My personality was different, much less outgoing than hers. Even so, her words convicted me. There was, indeed, self-pity in my heart. God gave me the grace to confess it and receive forgiveness. When tempted again to self-pity, and it happened often, I reminded myself that Tante Corrie was paying a far harder price physically than I was paying and as close as I was becoming to her I continued to see no hint of self-pity. She really lived her message.

The weeks passed quickly and Tante Corrie saw to it that I added to my wardrobe some brightly colored dresses. Some of our hostesses suggested that my very pale coloring would be enhanced by the use of blush and lipstick and helped me choose some suitable items. By the time we reached Hawaii with its soporific and humid heat, I decided that Tante Corrie had been quite right in her evaluation that my long hair would be hard to deal with when traveling. In Honolulu I found a beauty shop and asked the hairdresser to cut it short. The result was surprisingly liberating. Tante Corrie viewed the effect with obvious satisfaction. "I am proud of my daughter," she said.

A deep bond was developing between Tante Corrie and me and while I still regarded myself as her temporary helper I knew it would not be easy to find a substitute. We were traveling constantly. How could we find out about the gifts of any prospective companion/nurse if we never settled down for more than a few days? There was the added factor that a companion would be at a great disadvantage if she did not speak Dutch. I had a sneaking feeling that Tante Corrie was expecting me to stay on with her. She referred to future work as though I would still be with her.

Several months after I had joined her we were once again in Southern California. This was not only to fulfill speaking engagements, but also to meet with her Board of Directors, called "Christians Incorporated," under the leadership of Bill and Bettie Butler whom I knew from my first visit to the States on behalf of Brother Andrew. Bill and Bettie worked out the schedule of coming speaking engagements and did a great deal of organization on her behalf. It was good to have time to spend with them in planning.

But while we were in California I also knew that the time had come when I had to make a choice. If I was to leave her, Tante Corrie would need to make definite arrangements for a replacement. I could not remain on temporary assignment from Brother Andrew's ministry. He needed to know where I stood and his presence in Southern California for speaking engagements reminded me that I had to come to a decision.

It was while we were at a hotel in Anaheim, California,

that one day, leaving Tante Corrie in the company of a visitor, I went for a walk. It was mid-summer, and very hot. The pavement felt warm through my shoes and the smoggy air had its usual acrid smell. When I looked up at the palms, one of the few things of beauty in the concrete labyrinth, the polluted air caused me to see the fronds as if through a veil. I was glad we would be moving on soon. I had stayed not far from here during my trip four years earlier and had returned to Holland with the impression that I would not like to live in Southern California. That feeling was even more strongly underlined now.

As I walked rather aimlessly through Anaheim's hot smog, I prayed for guidance. The thought of continued travel was daunting, but so was the thought of abandoning Tante Corrie. I liked to walk and pray. The forward movement of it helped me, and so, especially, did the solitude. Even though the area was densely populated there were very few walkers. Hundreds of cars flashed by, their windows carefully rolled up against the smoggy heat. As I walked I became convinced that the right thing to do was to continue with Tante Corrie and give my notice to Brother Andrew. It was with a peaceful feeling of relief that I made the choice.

Was it really a choice, I asked myself, or was I simply following an ordained plan that became clear to me as I learned to surrender? I did not have to continue with this kind of life. I could at any point refuse to surrender. But then I would miss the life He had prepared me. It was awesome to think that I, as we all can do, was cooperating with the living God.

It was not an easy thing to give notice to Brother Andrew whose ministry had been part of my life for so long. But I knew that the message of the suffering Church would always remain with me and there might be ways to help them in the future about which I did not yet know.

As Tante Corrie and I packed our suitcases once again for the next stage of the journey, I knew that my decision to stay with her was a lot more than just an agreement to help an old lady. I remembered how as a teenager in England, before I gave my life to the Lord Jesus, I had three big objections to Christian service. I had thought that laying down my life for Jesus' sake might mean leaving England. It had. But how much I had gained in doing it. My second objection had been that I could never speak in public. God's way for me had required that I did. And I had discovered that I could, and that people listened.

But what about the third objection? As a teenager I had said that I would not be single for the Lord's sake. But after I had surrendered my life to Him, He had so far required that of me too. And although He had enabled me to live a full and satisfied life, I had always hoped that the time would come when singleness would no longer be a requirement. Now, though, I was joining my life to that of a lady who, in spite of the limitations of her age, was physically tough. She might live for many years. Would that mean a life commitment to her? And would the passing years mean that I would give up all the chances of marriage and a home? I did not know. But I now knew enough about God to be able to tell myself that His way was best. "No good thing," I reminded myself, "does He withhold from those whose walk is blameless." And by blameless, I was coming to feel He meant ". . . those who are yielded." Because I was His, He would always give me what was best.

A few weeks later as I scanned a list, provided by Bill and Bettie Butler, of cities where Tante Corrie was to speak next, I came across a strange name: Waco, Texas.

Wherever was that, and how should it be pronounced? Delving to the bottom of the black attaché case, which was my traveling office, I retrieved a book of maps and found Texas. Waco was about a hundred miles south of Dallas, where our plane was to land. The schedule informed me that we were to be met by a Dr. and Mrs. Charles Shellenberger. I looked forward to the visit to Texas, although I did hope I'd be able to understand the Texas drawl.

So it was that in late September 1976, our plane landed in Dallas. At the gate Tante Corrie and I were met by a good-looking middle-aged couple. Dr. Shellenberger was tall, sandy haired, with spectacles and a very engaging smile. Mrs. Shellenberger was my height, I judged, with white hair and beautiful brown eyes. They soon insisted that we call them by their first names, Charles and Dorothy. Dorothy seemed to share with me a love for drama judging by her word choice and vivid descriptions. She also loved beauty. That was clear from her report that during this next couple of days we could expect to observe the migration of tens of thousands of monarch butterflies as they made their way across this part of Texas. We might even see some during our two-hour drive to their city of Waco.

About halfway to Waco our hosts turned into a roadside rest stop, hauled a large hamper from the back of the car, and suggested that we have a picnic. Tante Corrie and I were delighted. It had been a long time since we had enjoyed a casual outside meal. I looked in vain for monarch butterflies as I consumed my sandwiches and fruit, my gaze taking in what seemed to be hundreds of miles of Texas plains, broken here and there by small, wiry-looking trees. The scene was bathed in a golden autumn light. What was there about this landscape that was light and familiar? And then I knew. It reminded me of the flat country of Holland with its remarkably clear light where I had spent many happy years. This was something like coming home.

Charles and Dorothy drove us to a large, one-story, cozy house and installed Tante Corrie and me in separate bedrooms. We soon learned that, having been a pediatrician in the city for the best part of thirty years, Charles was greatly loved and seemed to know a large portion of the population. Although he was very busy with his daily work, he also paid a great deal of attention to his elderly guest and her companion.

Soon Dorothy shared with us the remarkable way in which she had been introduced to Tante Corrie. In 1972 she had been admitted to a hospital suffering severe depression. Her doctor had told Charles that she would have to take medication for the rest of her life. Eventually she was discharged from the hospital, still far from well. On the day she was brought home she found on her coffee table a copy of *The Hiding Place*. She read it, then again and again, in all eight times. It was a major factor in her eventual complete healing. She was never able to find out how the book arrived on her coffee table. But since then she had had a special love for Tante Corrie and had used her speaking and acting skills to tell the book's story to groups large and small.

Tante Corrie worked hard in Waco, speaking at three meetings, including one at Baylor University. The Shellenbergers, probably sensing that I was in need of rest, did all they could to provide it, including the arranging of an afternoon outing with a young couple. We took bikes and cycled for miles in the late September sun in a large park near Waco's Brazos River. The stay in this home and city was a gift from God of deep refreshment for me, so much so that I surprised myself by recording in my diary as the time for our departure approached, "I don't want to leave here."

Neither, I suspected, did Tante Corrie. Lately she had been talking more and more about the possibility of having her own home in the United States. Traveling was obviously very tiring for her now. And a new U.S. government ruling made it impossible for us to renew our visitors' visas for longer than three months at a time. In order for Tante Corrie to work in the United States, we would need to apply for permanent resident status. She began to see that this was the time to seek a permanent place to live within the United States and she prayed for it earnestly. She told me she believed that the most practical place for her to settle down would be near her Board, in Southern California.

I wondered whether or not she would be happy living in one place. And could I ever get used to living in that fast-moving, smog-enclosed society? I did not know that the pursuing of the idea to have her own home was going to usher in an unusual and very mysterious time of ministry.

Chapter Eight

A Struggling Servant

At the end of October 1976, Tante Corrie and I boarded a jet at Chicago's O'Hare International Airport, bound for Holland. Seven months of intensive travel lay behind us and I spent many hours of our trans-Atlantic journey reflecting on all I had learned since I first arrived on Tante Corrie's doorstep. Shy, yet independent and not too keen to share my life with her, I soon learned that although she was devoted to the carrying out of her ministry, her interest in her helper was a deep and real one, and it was now quite natural to share my mail and many of my thoughts with her. And much more than that, we had become a team. I wholeheartedly believed in her and her ministry.

I had seen many things during this past half-year that had caused my admiration to rise. Tante Corrie had kept all her promises to speak and in spite of fatigue and weakness had never given in to self-pity. That helped me in my own struggles with tiredness and homesickness. I had also seen that her love for people and her acceptance of their demands on her were not just a result of her outgoing personality. It was because she was rightly related to the Lord Jesus, like a mirror hanging in the right direction and doing its job, that she was able to reflect His love to them. And I had learned that when she taught she used very simple examples and spoke in story form. What power there was, I thought, in a good story. There seemed to be a basic drive in men and women to listen. God was taking the truths she portrayed and by the power of the Holy Spirit was changing people's lives. I felt fulfilled. The Lord's way this past eleven years had not always been easy, but the knowledge that I was doing work He had prepared in advance for me to do satisfied me at the deepest level of my being.

On arrival in Holland we set to work at once. My first task, now that I had decided to stay on indefinitely with Corrie ten Boom and to move to America with her, was to return to Harderwijk, pack my belongings, and put them in storage. I stayed in the area for a couple of days, taking the opportunity to tell my former colleagues all about my adventures and to say goodbye to my friends. Next Tante Corrie and I got in touch with the United States Consul in Rotterdam. After we had completed many formalities we were eventually issued small, laminated pieces of paper— our "green cards." These would enable us to stay in the United States as resident aliens. Now we could really turn our attention to a permanent home in the United States.

First, though, at Tante Corrie's urging, I paid a visit to England. I wondered how my family was. We had been in touch through letters, but how were they really? What would happen if there were some family crisis and I was far away?

Leaving Tante Corrie in the capable hands of Riska, my former colleague in Brother Andrew's office, and who on returning from mission work in Nepal had taken care of Tante Corrie's home base, I flew to England and a joyous reunion with my parents, grandmother, Sylvia, Bruce, their two children, Digger, his wife, and their two children.

My parents now no longer lived in the red-brick house near the park gates. They had moved to a small house on the cliffs overlooking the English Channel, Dad's elderly mother's home, so they could take care of her. Dad had retired this past summer from his work of more than forty years with the local government. Mother still worked at the Royal East Sussex Hospital, now as a clinical instructor in the School of Nursing.

I was as proud as ever of my mother, sixty now. Her delightful, sunny personality made her a joy to be with. There was a serenity to her life that had increased with her years. Dad had always given her every opportunity to follow her nursing career. She was a fulfilled woman. I had greatly missed her during the past seven months in the United States, but her long epistles had reached me each week ever since I had first left England ten years before, even while I was traveling. And now that I was home in England, Mother questioned me in interested detail about my time with Tante Corrie.

Near the end of my stay in England, the Lord brought home to me very unexpectedly that I did not need to worry about being in the wrong place when my family needed me.

Mother and I were chatting in the back room overlooking the English Channel one mid-afternoon when the telephone rang with news that her only brother, to whom she was devoted, had died at work in Wales just a half-hour previously. Dad was in another town and could not be reached, my brother and sister were with their families. The Lord had arranged it for Mother to have me with her when the distressing news came. I tried to help her as much as I could, thanking God for this remarkable timing.

I had no idea that there would be another occasion in the future when my mother needed me and when I would be even more thankful to God for His care-filled timing.

Back in Holland, I found Tante Corrie eager to finalize our affairs and return to the United States. She was sure that the Lord would give her a home in California. I had some misgivings, however. What would it be like to be confined in a house? And near smoggy Los Angeles at that?

But I tried to enter into Tante Corrie's excitement as once again we packed our suitcases. She was nearly 85 now and I had noticed a slowing down recently. She needed to take several short naps during the day and she was often breathless and pale. *So, Tante Corrie,* I said to myself, *you are going to your own home in California although we do not know where it is yet. Will you ever come back to your homeland?* I did not voice my thoughts to Tante Corrie. If she had any premonition that she would never see Holland again, she did not mention it.

Before we could go to America, we flew to Sweden where Billy Graham had invited Tante Corrie to give her testimony at one of his meetings. A young woman, Glenda, part of the advance team, was a great help to us and before we left she told us that she would keep in touch. It was one of thousands of apparently chance meetings, but a time would come, years later, when Glenda would be used to help me find my way into another of the works God had prepared beforehand that I should walk in.

Tante Corrie talked more and more often now about her new home. "Oh child," she would say, "it will be good not to travel anymore. Let's look for a single-story house. It must not be too expensive. And let's not be too far from our Board's office in Orange. I want to make filmed messages of all my talks so that they can travel and I do not have to. And I want to write several more books. We will make a cozy home and have lots of visitors. I want to be able to receive visitors who are invalids, so let's have a house with no steps. And let's have a lot of flowers in the yard outside, and birdfeeders."

"Yes, Tante Corrie," was my usual reply, but I held my breath. Tante Corrie was planning a dazzlingly busy life, even if it did not include much travel. Would we really be able to have a home that in any way could be called normal? Would not constant visitors interrupt her writing plans? And how ever could I run a house and be her secretary, driver, and companion? Housework had never appealed to me much and I was rather proud of the fact that I had reached my early thirties with a minimum of cooking experience. Cooking was not my calling. I had decided that long ago . . . and so, I was certain, had others!

Finally we were on our way to Los Angeles Airport where we were met by the executive officers of Tante Corrie's Board. The Butlers told Tante Corrie that they had been in touch with a realtor who would take us on a tour of possible homes; then they drove us to a hotel in Anaheim, where we installed ourselves for an indefinite period. Looking through the hotel window I saw that once again the palm trees were shrouded in gray veils. Orange County was as smoggy as ever.

February 1977 was very hot in Anaheim and the next days held some discouraging moments. Accompanied by a realtor we visited many houses. If the floor plan was just right, the price was too high. Many were in an unsuitable location. Tante Corrie became increasingly tired, and both of us were disappointed. Back in our hotel room we prayed much that we would soon be led to the right house. Tante Corrie suggested that we study *Spiritual Depression—Its*

Causes and Cure by D. Martyn Lloyd-Jones, and as we read we found ourselves encouraged by the chapter that dealt with trials. The passage we were asked to consider was 1 Peter 1:6–7: "In this you greatly rejoice, though now for a little while you may have had to suffer grief in all kinds of trials. These have come so that your faith—of greater worth than gold, which perishes even though refined by fire—may be proved genuine and may result in praise, glory and honor when Jesus Christ is revealed."

Two things from that passage helped us in our particular trial of not being able to find a suitable home. First, the words "now for a little while." This trial would not go on forever. And then we noticed the words "you may have to." There was a purpose in this trial. God knew that it was necessary. We reminded ourselves that He often allows people to go through trials just before they undertake a work for Him.

At that thought Tante Corrie's spirits revived. She loved work. I told myself again that the important thing for me to remember was that the work came first. The Lord was giving us a house in order that we undertake a work. But I also believed that He would give us a place to enjoy and in which to feel at home. When and where would it be?

We did not have to wait much longer. Soon two friends who had purchased a home for rental purposes in the city of Placentia offered it to Tante Corrie at standard rent. They told her that she could stay in the house for as long or short a time as she wished and if she did not like it, could use it as her base while she continued her search.

We went to view the house. I do not know what I had been anticipating, but I was rather disappointed. The house was nondescript from the outside. There was a room with a large picture window on the right-hand side, on the left was a garage, and in between was a walkway leading to a cream and brown front door. At the back we found a rectangular yard, with a sandbox and swings from previous tenants. I felt a twinge at the children's playthings, remembering for a moment how I had longed for a home of my own.

Inside, the house was gloomy. The floors were covered with shag carpet in an ugly shade of avocado green. The wallpaper in the living room had a heavy gold design, rather more suitable for a ballroom, I thought, than for Corrie ten Boom's main reception room. The dining room to the left had walls with a more acceptable color and the kitchen, with a cheerful floral pattern, in yellow, was quite nice. All the rooms in the main part of the house were dark. Although there were sliding glass doors along the length of the dining and living rooms, a patio of heavy wood adjoining them cut out most of the light.

I was astonished, though, at Tante Corrie's reaction. As soon as she stepped over the threshold she acted as if it were home. It was not far from the office in Orange, and did not have steps. The rent was acceptable. She was seeing the house that was going to be, not the house that was. I knew the search was over when Tante Corrie told me she would like to place her desk in the living room in front of the sliding glass doors.

So suddenly I had to start looking at the house with different eyes. At the back of the house, overlooking the swingset, was a bedroom that would be mine. Next to it were two smaller rooms. These would be suitable as an office and guest room. Finally, at the front of the house, we found a large bedroom with its own bathroom and lots of storage space. It faced east and was quite the lightest room so far. This was definitely the bedroom for Tante Corrie.

I should have known from her homes in Holland that Tante Corrie's first priority in this house would be light and color. With the owners' permission the ugly wallpaper was removed from the living room and replaced by magnolia-colored paint. My bedroom also received paint in place of its child's wallpaper, and so did the office. We borrowed and bought beds, desks, tables, and chairs. Many Orange County churches, hearing that Tante Corrie was moving nearby, held showers for her. There were bedroom, bathroom, dining room, patio, and kitchen showers. Soon the house had all it needed in the way of basic equipment and more. It even had a television set and record player. We planted pink and red roses and baby grapefruit, orange, and lemon trees.

On February 28, 1977, Tante Corrie moved into her new home, "Shalom House." I had never seen her so happy. From the time she got up until the time she went to bed, she expressed her joy at being able to sleep with her head on the same pillow every night after more than three decades of travel.

Which only meant that Tante Corrie was now ready to go to work. She called a meeting of her Board of Directors. For a couple of hours she laid her plans and hopes before her Board. She wanted to write five books and to make five filmed messages. She wanted to do more for prisoners, since she too had been a prisoner. She hoped to conduct radio and magazine interviews from her home. She wanted to make her books available to Christians in Eastern Europe. And of course she would be receiving guests. Although I had now been with her for nearly a year, she still amazed me with her energy and drive. This was Tante Corrie at her best. She loved life and she loved work.

I was impressed at the way her Board members listened, made suggestions, gave her their wholehearted backing. Tante Corrie went to bed early that night, but she was happy. As for me, I went to bed with mixed feelings. The amount of work facing us seemed overwhelming.

And indeed it nearly proved to be. Over a month of typing manuscripts and letters, talking on the telephone, receiving guests, and trying to run the household, even with the help of part-time volunteers, proved too much for me.

One day in late March, after a tearful weekend, I knew that I had to have a few days' break. Board member Ed Elfstrom and his wife, Thelma, offered me hospitality at their home in Fullerton. There, in the quiet of the beautiful bedroom allotted to me, I tried to pull myself together.

The trouble was clear. I had become a servant. Years before, when I had given my life to the Lord, I told Him I wanted to serve Him—but *this* wasn't what I meant! I was a typist and maid. Everything was wrong. I hated the plasticness of Southern California, its smog and its fast pace. I did *not* like being a 24-hour beck-and-call servant. And I did *not* like being constantly on the run, as if we had to hurry before the world itself came to an end.

But there it was. I tried submitting my will to the Lord's again that weekend but I did not receive the peace that had always followed. It was as if some element were missing.

There were practical answers to my work overload that helped, at least at one level. The Lord sent us Riska, whose lively presence was a big encouragement. And then when Riska returned to Holland, Elizabeth Burson, white-haired and motherly, came to Shalom House as part-time housekeeper and we engaged the weekly services of a gardener. As important as these extra hands were, it still seemed to me that an air of time pressure hung over our household, which I had never known in my year-and-a-half with Tante Corrie. What was it all about?

Hints began to come. In the living room against the wall

behind Tante Corrie's desk was a white sectional sofa and she and I often sat there together during the evening hours. She liked to do needlework and although I did not find it particularly satisfying I tried my hand at a few patterns. She also read a great deal and we talked often. But there came a time when communication was threatened. She could not understand me very well and kept asking me to repeat sentences. I knew this was a combination of two things—my own soft voice and the fact that she was experiencing an increasing loss of hearing. I suspected that her loss of hearing was the greater problem, but at first Tante Corrie did not see it as such. It was perhaps a small matter but the extra effort of trying to make myself understood did nothing to ease my work load.

After many requests that I raise my voice to what was, for me, an uncomfortable level, I suggested we try an experiment. I would make an appointment with an expert in speech and hearing at the University of California in Fullerton. If he discovered that my lack of volume was simply laziness I would do all I could to correct it. Tante Corrie agreed.

The day came when I returned from my campus appointment feeling relieved, and yet apprehensive. The speech expert had told me that I had a naturally very soft voice. He compared its volume to the weight of a butterfly and told me that there was not much I could do to improve it. *Well,* I said to myself, *that leaves one solution. Tante Corrie should have her ears tested. But will she accept that?*

I need not have worried. Coming into the house, I gave Tante Corrie a full report of the speech expert's findings.

"All right," was her immediate response, "I will get a hearing aid."

And she did, without delay. My respect for her rose still

higher. Tante Corrie was not too proud to accept the help of a hearing aid. She was willing to undertake anything that was necessary for the sake of the work. Very soon the new instrument was part of her life.

And still the sense of pressure mounted. Why did Tante Corrie have to see so many visitors? Although many of the people who came to Shalom House were there for good reasons—to receive counsel, to advise Tante Corrie on her books, to help with many projects—I had the feeling that many came just because they wanted to meet a famous person. I had a sense of who really needed help and who, as I saw it, wanted to use the contact with her for their own ends. Once, when after a very busy day, two men showed up at the door and after drinking tea with her, wanted me to photograph them with her in the garden, I felt like refusing. I had a suspicion that they wanted to display the photograph and thus give a boost to their own ministry. Could they not see that this elderly lady was tired? Why had they barged in on our day unannounced?

I talked to Tante Corrie about it later, but she had no complaint. "Child, if it helps their work it does not matter," was her reply. There it was again. The work of the Kingdom always came first and for its sake she was willing to be used.

I wished that I could feel the urgent need to take advantage of every situation, as did Tante Corrie. She never seemed to feel that she was being used; I had to admit that I often did.

For example, there was the Sunday afternoon when I was looking forward to some peace and quiet. It was a beautiful day and I decided that I would put on my swimsuit, take a book, and lie in the back yard. It seemed that no sooner was I settled than the telephone rang and on answering it, Tante Corrie found herself speaking to an old missionary friend. Telling her that she would be welcome to afternoon tea, Tante Corrie asked me to get changed and ready for the visit. *Oh, well,* I thought, as I made my way to the kitchen to prepare yet another tray of tea. *When Tante Corrie told me at my interview that the work comes first she obviously meant it. I cannot say that I was not warned.*

All the pressure to get work done was bearing fruit for Tante Corrie. She was able to make progress on many of the projects she had outlined to her Board on arrival in Shalom House. Two manuscripts were completed and she had worked on filming some of her talks. She was invited to visit San Quentin prison and her longing to help prisoners was thus partly fulfilled.

Then, one weekend in August, six months after we started this unusually heavy work push, I was spending a day in Fullerton at the home of Mr. and Mrs. Elfstrom. The order and quietness of their home did a lot to restore my strength and perspective. I had decided to try to regard this part of God's plan for my life as a marathon and prayed constantly for strength to continue. I thought it unnecessary for Tante Corrie to work as hard as she did and often suggested that she slow down. It was not that she did not listen to me. She did, but she did not take my advice. *Anybody would think, Tante Corrie, that you are racing against the clock,* I said to myself.

And then I started at my own words.

Perhaps she was.

One of our discussions in the evening light on the sofa in the living room had to do with marriage.

"Are you content not to be married?" Tante Corrie asked me one evening at coffee time.

"Well, yes, Tante Corrie," I replied. "I would like to be,

one day, but so far the Lord has not led me into marriage. I am glad I can be with you."

I told her the story, which, although she had heard it many times, she always seemed to like to hear again about the three reasons why, as a teenager, I had not wanted to surrender my life to God's service. He might want me to go abroad. He might want me to speak in public. He might want me to be single for His sake. He had asked all those things of me, but I could tell Tante Corrie that I truly had no regrets even though it often was not easy.

"A good marriage is one of the most joyous things in the world," said Tante Corrie, "and a bad marriage is one of the worst things in the world." And then she reminisced.

"I had a boyfriend once," she said. "When I was a young woman in Holland a pastoral student named Karel became interested in me and I believed that he intended for us to become engaged, even though my brother knew Karel's family and had told me that they wanted him to marry well. Our family was poor, but I reckoned that Karel was old enough to know his own mind and I was sure he loved me.

"One day he arrived at our house with a young woman and introduced her to me and the family as his fiancée. That news was shattering to me. As soon as they left I went to my room and wept. God gave me the grace to surrender Karel to Him, but it was not easy. But instead God has given me a life of joy and fulfillment."

I was touched at Tante Corrie's telling about her boyfriend of many decades earlier. I remembered that there was a chapter about her and Karel in the book *The Hiding Place* and before I went to sleep that night I reread it. I particularly noted the advice her father gave her when he found the young Corrie sobbing on her bed.

"Corrie, do you know what hurts so very much? It's

love. Love is the strongest force in the world, and when it is blocked that means pain.

"There are two things we can do when this happens. We can kill the love so that it stops hurting. But then of course part of us dies, too. Or, Corrie, we can ask God to open up another route for that love to travel."

I thought about how Tante Corrie's surrender of Karel and of her right to marriage had resulted in a very fruitful life. God had opened up another route for her love to travel and had given her His perfect way. And I had to believe that this difficult way that I was now taking was also His perfect way for me.

One day soon afterward I received an unusual request. A local couple with whom we were acquainted was keen that I should meet a young man of about my age and asked if they could take me out to dinner with him. I thought about it for a while. Was this what the Americans called a "date"? I had not been out with a man for nearly ten years. What should I wear and how should I behave? In the end I decided it could not do any harm and accepted the invitation. Tante Corrie was agreeable to my going and it was arranged that I would be picked up by the couple early one evening. I chose to wear an informal blouse and skirt.

I was curious about the "date" whom we were to meet at the couple's house before proceeding to a small restaurant near the beach. He seemed nice enough. Dark-haired, not very tall, and a few years older than I, he had a friendly, outgoing personality. We drove down to the beach and the four of us enjoyed a good fish meal in a quiet and rather exclusive restaurant. About halfway through the evening, I heard my date talking about a woman who had evidently been part of his past. And then

I realized he was referring to his ex-wife. This man was divorced.

After the meal our hosts drove the four of us back to their home and the date suggested taking me on to Shalom House in his car. On the way he told me that he would like to see more of me. I tried to keep my answer vague and just before getting out of the car told him I would think about it.

But inside I had already made up my mind much earlier in the evening, as soon as I had heard him refer to his ex-wife. There was no point in my developing a relationship with a divorced man. Relationships can lead to marriage and I knew that I would not consider marrying anybody who had been married before and whose marriage had ended in anything other than the death of his wife. *I have kept myself for one man,* I told myself, *and if ever I am to marry, I want it to be his first marriage too.*

Used by now to sharing my experiences and thoughts with Tante Corrie, I told her all about the evening, and my conclusions, which she seemed to receive with some relief. It was as though she was thinking that our busy life did not have room for the complication of a boyfriend. And I knew that she was right.

One day Tante Corrie, who liked to read whenever she had the opportunity, was immersed in a Dutch book about wartime experiences. I was making a cup of coffee for us when I heard her exclaim and then come toward the kitchen. "I have found something very interesting," she said. "Karel is mentioned in this book. It tells that he was incarcerated in the war and that he took a firm stand against the Nazis. Isn't that wonderful?"

I agreed that it was. I did not question her further about her boyfriend of many decades earlier and did not know whether this was the first news she had had of him. But I remembered the words of her father after the distressing news came that Karel was engaged to a wealthy young woman: "God loves Karel—even more than you do—and if you ask Him, He will give you His love for this man, a love nothing can prevent, nothing destroy. Whenever we cannot love in the old, human way, Corrie, God can give us the perfect way."

In her mid-eighties, Corrie ten Boom was still displaying the right kind of love for Karel. She was delighting in the fact that he had taken brave action in the war. There were no sour feelings toward him. Seeing in Tante Corrie the effect, decades later, of true surrender, I wanted to commit wholly to God, yet again, the deep feelings, vibrant and yet dormant, for a man who, if he existed, was as yet unknown to me. And once again I did.

As the busy months continued I was very grateful for the help of Elizabeth Burson. She did not live in the house and worked part-time, but I could not have coped without her and without many local volunteers who helped with typing, receiving of guests, household repairs, sewing, and additional cooking. So far I had not had to do much housework myself. Before she left us each Friday, Elizabeth usually prepared meals that could be heated up for Saturday and Sunday.

Tante Corrie and I tried to keep Sundays as quiet as possible. Because she was so well-known we did not have a regular church, but visited several, including Rose Drive Friends Church in nearby Yorba Linda, whose members provided us with a large amount of volunteer help. And when she did not go to church, Tante Corrie liked to listen to the radio broadcast of Chuck Smith from Calvary Chapel of Costa Mesa.

She was especially delighted when, one day at the end of August 1977, a telephone call brought me the news from Bruce, Sylvia's husband, that I had become aunt to twin boys, Nathaniel and Daniel Baker. They had been born prematurely but both were well, and so was Sylvia. Tante Corrie was as happy with the news as I was. When would I be able to meet my new nephews?

There was seldom a let-up in the work, but Tante Corrie did all she could to see that my needs were met. She urged me to join a local gym and work out as often as possible. She saw to it that I had at least one day off each week and continued to show much interest in my family. In the autumn, knowing that it would be possible for us to find somebody to stay with her for a few weeks, she insisted that I make plans to visit my family in England.

But then, just when a suitable volunteer had been found to stay with her and all plans for my departure were ready, it became necessary for Tante Corrie to enter the hospital for the insertion of a pacemaker. She had become increasingly tired and short of breath and a visit to a heart specialist revealed that her heart was beating at a very low rate. The doctor told Tante Corrie that she probably would not live long without surgery to implant a pacemaker.

This placed her in a dilemma. On the one hand she very much wanted to go to heaven. On the other hand there was work for her to do. And her friends and I urged her to have the surgery as soon as possible. We did not want to lose her. Tante Corrie told me that she felt as though she had a choice—to go to heaven or to stay on earth. She decided to have surgery and entered the hospital on October 6, 1977. The operation, performed without general anesthetic, was difficult for her and afterward she told me that at one time she thought she could bear the pain no longer. "And then," she said, "I saw a hand pierced by a nail and I could thank the Lord Jesus for the far worse pain He suffered for my sins. It made me quiet and thankful. I

kept thinking of His love and His suffering and kept looking at that hand and He gave me the strength to come
through."

After a week in the hospital, now with a heartbeat no
lower than 72 per minute, Tante Corrie quickly gained
strength and urged me not to cancel my trip home. Leaving her in the care of a friend, I flew to England, first
visiting the south coast and enjoying a good reunion with
Mother and Dad and my brother and his family.

And then I traveled north, to Mottram near Manchester,
to see for myself the little village where Sylvia and Bruce
were now living, and to meet the members of the small
independent evangelical church of which Bruce was pastor. I received a very loving welcome from the church and
was given the opportunity to tell about my life in the
United States. I found the culture very different from that
of the south of England. People were more open and
friendly. Many spoke with the broad accents of Lancashire
and Cheshire. Mottram was built on the edge of the moors.
I could not help comparing their landscape to that of Holland. While Holland had a bright kind of light, the moors
had a dark light. There was something brooding about the
wildness, which I could see from Sylvia's kitchen window.

But there was little time to reflect on the moors. Sylvia's
household was as busy as Shalom House. I delighted in
my beautiful twin nephews, Nathaniel and Daniel, two
months old. I gave Sylvia as much help as I could with
them and with Gideon and Naomi, their older brother and
sister for whom this aunt they rarely saw must have been
something of a mystery.

One day when there was an unusual time of quiet, little
Gideon and I were in the sitting room together and he
asked me a question.

"You are not married, are you, Auntie Pammy?" His

blond curly head was cocked to the right and his gray eyes regarded me with deep interest.

"No, Gideon," I replied, rather startled. The question had been put to me often, but never by a four-year-old.

"Why aren't you married, Auntie Pammy?" was Gideon's next question. I had been asked that often, too, and was never sure of the answer. Was it that I had never met the right person? Or was it more correct to say that God had not yet allowed it? I was not used to dealing with children's questions and sought the right answer more carefully.

"The Lord has not told me to, Gideon," I replied finally. "Not for now."

Straightening his back, Gideon gave me a wide smile. "I will look after you!" he said. His tone was confident and reassuring.

I thanked him and decided to lock the incident in my memory. I would enjoy reminding him of it as he got older and teasing him. But it also touched me. I had not seen the children very often and yet, as young as he was, I felt that Gideon understood that the Lord had given me a special calling and was doing his part to encourage me. And from now on I had my answer to the frequently put and annoying question "Why are you not married?" I would always give the answer I had given to Gideon.

Although I was greatly enjoying my time in England, half of me was anxious to get back to Placentia and Tante Corrie who wrote frequently keeping me up-to-date with events in Shalom House and telling me that she was looking forward to welcoming me home to California again. The separation from her for nearly three weeks underlined to me that I loved her very much and, as hard as it sometimes was, that I was very glad that the Lord had given me the task to stand with her at this time in her life.

Soon the time in England was over and I waved goodbye to my family. I had no inkling that it would be a long time before I could visit my homeland again.

Back in Placentia, I was glad to see that Tante Corrie had recovered well from her pacemaker operation. Her color was good, her energy level stronger. She was working as hard as ever.

During the next months she saw many of her desires fulfilled. Three books, *Jesus is Victor—He Cares, He Comforts; Jesus is Victor—He Sets the Captive Free;* and *Each New Day*, a devotional, were completed and published. And a great deal of time was spent in filming her messages. Traveling to locations in Arizona and Los Angeles County she spent many tiring hours under the direction of her friend Jim Collier whom she had come to know during the filming of "The Hiding Place." She made a film for prisoners, one for Indians, and one called "Jesus is Victor—a personal portrait of Corrie ten Boom."

These tangible results of all her efforts made Tante Corrie very happy. One evening we were ending the day together in her bedroom at the front of Shalom House. She had asked me to open the window and to draw back the drapes as soon as I had turned out the light. Tante Corrie was lying in her double bed with its dark wood headboard and I was sitting on the edge of the bed. Together we thanked the Lord for all He had allowed her to accomplish in writing books and making films while at Shalom House. After she had said Amen, which she always pronounced loudly and definitely, she opened her eyes and looked at me with an expression I could only describe as profound satisfaction.

"Child," she said, "always be sure you know what you are asking when you pray because the Lord hears and the Lord answers."

After saying goodnight to Tante Corrie and turning out the light, I went to my room thoughtfully. I had to admit that once again I was finding my role very difficult. It was sometimes hard to know how to pray. I often asked simply for strength, but that was such a general prayer. I wished that I could find more balance in my life with Tante Corrie. On the one hand I was glad I was with her. On the other hand I still often found myself balking at my servant role. Why could I not reach a place of consistent peace? Was I really in the right place?

One day soon afterward, wanting to settle the question once and for all, I left Tante Corrie in housekeeper Elizabeth's care and made for the coast, a drive of about forty minutes. There was something about the ocean that was familiar and soothing. Perhaps it was because I had grown up within sight of the English Channel that I liked to drive to the coast as often as I could. Taking a deck chair I set it up on a cliff overlooking the Pacific. It was a warm, clear day. Splashes of color on semi-tropical trees and bushes caught my eye everywhere. Palm trees waved overhead. The rush of traffic was far away. I closed my eyes. I felt calmer already.

"Lord," I prayed, "I am confused. I can see that You have guided me clearly to be with Tante Corrie, yet although I love her, I am often unhappy in my role. I do not like being a servant. Please help me to come to a place of acceptance or please show me if I am in the wrong place."

I sat in silence for a few minutes and then it seemed as if the Lord spoke to me inside and what He said was something like this:

I want you to take a look at a typical day in Shalom House and then try to view it from a heavenly perspective.

So I ran a mental film of a day in Shalom House, viewing it on the screen of my eyelids closed against the bright Pacific sun.

I saw Tante Corrie as I took tea to her in her bedroom early in the morning and heard her plans for the coming day. I saw her greeting her Board members and making important decisions. I saw her enjoying her garden with its rosebushes and birdfeeders. Answering telephone calls. Dictating correspondence. Writing her manuscripts. I saw the fatigue in her face and her frequent naps. I remembered her love and concern for me and how on my birthday recently she came to my room early in the morning with roses from her garden and two cups of tea. I saw her dependence on the help of others.

And then on the cliff overlooking the ocean, I opened my eyes. It was as though I suddenly saw things from God's point of view. Here was a warrior who had worked very hard but who was slowing down. God had provided a home for her in which she was deeply happy and in which she could work hard. I saw anew how kind God was. And then I saw something else. He had provided the home not only for her, but for me, too. He wanted me to see His kindness when His children come to the end of their lives. I knew that the matter was settled. However, off balance I might feel in the future with my servant role there must be no question of my leaving her. I was in the right place whether or not I was always happy.

And then I prayed something that I think up until then I had been afraid to pray. It was another prayer of surrender but it was different from simply relinquishing present circumstances into the hands of God. It opened up the way, in faith, for Him to do anything He wanted in my life, but in a new way.

"Lord," I said, "whatever it takes to make me a more

godly woman, will You bring it to pass?" It was as honest a prayer as I knew how to form.

And then I remembered Tante Corrie's words to me: Be careful that you know what you are asking, because God hears prayer and God answers.

God was about to allow something to happen that would test every word of my prayer.

Chapter Nine

Standing Still

As our second summer in Shalom House approached, nobody had a hint that Corrie ten Boom's public ministry was entering its final stage.

On the surface everything seemed to be going so well. Tante Corrie and I looked forward to receiving some very special guests. June 1978 was to see the arrival of my parents for a stay of several weeks, and the next month Mrs. Lotte Reimeringer, a widow whom Tante Corrie had known for more than thirty years, was to arrive from Holland for a vacation.

We had lived in Placentia for sixteen months now. Shalom House had seen the completion of several manuscripts, opened its doors to movie crews on numerous occasions, and had received hundreds of guests. In every way it was a base for Tante Corrie's ministry, but it had also become home. While I still hated the smog and the fast pace of Southern California life, I was beginning to feel part of the local community and had made several good friends. In our backyard the little grapefruit, lemon, and orange trees we had planted on moving in last year had become firmly established and were even sporting some immature fruit. The red and pink roses had done very well, too, and we frequently picked blooms for Tante Corrie's desk and the dining table.

It was a joy to welcome my parents to our home and to introduce them to Tante Corrie who greeted them with love and made provision for me to spend much free time with them. Leaving her in the company of a volunteer companion, Mother, Dad, and I and a new friend, Ruth, even drove to the Grand Canyon and back. It meant a lot to me that my parents could witness our daily life in America. They soon saw that although life at Shalom House was very disciplined under Tante Corrie's leadership, we did not have a daily routine. I was proud of the way Mother and Dad pitched in to help with lots of odd jobs including the removal of all the furniture in the house so that the ugly avocado green shag floor covering could be replaced by light beige carpeting. At once it seemed as if there were much more light in the dark rooms, something I would deeply appreciate in the years lying ahead when very difficult circumstances would prevent my leaving Shalom House.

Unperturbed by visitors and new carpet, Tante Corrie was making an enthusiastic start on her publisher's latest challenge: a second daily devotional book to be entitled *This Day Is the Lord's*. No sooner had Lotte Reimeringer arrived from Holland in July than she began to assist Tante Corrie in research for the book. I learned quickly to have respect for Lotte who had taken a few weeks' break from her job as secretary at the Moravian Church's headquarters in The Netherlands. Before Tante Corrie had started her world travels in the 1940s, Lotte had been her secretary for a while. She was extremely good at languages, being fluent in Dutch, English, and German, and had a very loving way of dealing with Tante Corrie. In her late sixties, she was as tall as I, but more slightly built, which with her fair complexion gave her an almost delicate air. This, however, soon proved to be deceptive. As I watched Lotte take her share of cooking, receiving of guests, work on manuscripts, and foreign correspondence, I could see that she was used to hard work and quite capable of it. And I admired her for being willing to tackle so much during her vacation.

But the new devotional book could not be allowed to occupy all Tante Corrie's time. She also needed to prepare for a journey to Denver where in mid-July she was to receive an honor from Fleming H. Revell, her publisher, and World Wide Pictures, the filmmaking arm of the Billy Graham Association, producers of "The Hiding Place" movie. They had arranged for a special rendering of "This Is Your Life" with Tante Corrie as its subject to take place at the Christian Booksellers Association's convention. My parents and Lotte had also been invited to attend, and we all excitedly left for Denver.

Although her pacemaker had proved very beneficial to Tante Corrie's health since its insertion nine months before, the rarefied air of Denver caused chest pains and a portable tank of oxygen had to be delivered to our hotel room. This gave immediate relief and after two days of rest Tante Corrie much enjoyed being the subject of "This Is Your Life," receiving surprise guests from all over the U.S.A. and from Europe.

It was with a lightheartedness that we set out from Denver to Placentia. There, Tante Corrie went straight back to work on her new devotional book, enlisting Lotte's help whenever possible. The weather became extremely hot, but that did not cause a slowing down of Shalom House's busy schedule, nor of Tante Corrie's thoughtfulness.

One day the news reached us of the death of Karel,

whom Tante Corrie had once believed would become her husband. She asked Lotte to make inquiries about the address of his widow on her return to Holland, so that she could write a note of condolence. It was typical of her, although she was so busy, to do what she could to comfort Karel's widow in her loss. I thought again how her surrender to God of Karel and her right to marriage as a young woman had opened up the way for her to become a channel of God's love to countless people. It helped me to believe that my own surrender of my right to a husband and family would also somehow be used by God in the lives of others one day.

As the time for Lotte's return to Holland approached, Tante Corrie asked her to think about coming back to Placentia to help us on a full-time basis, particularly with her writing. Promising to consider this, Lotte boarded her plane for The Netherlands in mid-August and for the first time in many weeks, Tante Corrie and I were alone. There were no overnight guests and the daytime schedule was less heavy than usual.

For some reason I could not understand, Tante Corrie seemed a little downhearted. She was quiet and reflective and although she continued her habit of reporting on every incident there seemed to be some distance between us. I, too, found myself downhearted. The busy summer with its special guests and travel was behind us and we now had to give ourselves wholeheartedly to the work. There were no more outings in view and I told myself I would have to learn to be content behind the walls of Shalom House.

On August 21, Tante Corrie had a bad migraine headache, and when pain and nausea continued through the night she spent the next day in bed, sleeping for most of it, but feeling better in the evening. We talked and had our usual time of prayer before retiring early for the night.

The next morning when I rose about 7 A.M. the house was quiet. Looking from the door of my room up the corridor to Tante Corrie's room I saw through her open door that she had not drawn the heavy drapes yet, although she usually liked to watch the sunrise through her window facing east. I could not see Tante Corrie's bed, but knowing of her headaches of the past few days I imagined that she was still asleep. I went to the kitchen, made some tea, and took a cup with my Bible to the sitting room.

My reading that Wednesday morning was from John 13 and told about Jesus washing the disciples' feet. Peter protested. He did not understand why his Lord and Master should do such a thing. I was glad that there was a Peter in the Bible. There were so many ways in which I identified with him. He doubted and failed and spoke without thinking. And here he was not understanding true servanthood. I identified with him strongly. I had no inkling that the Lord was about to lead me into a lesson on servanthood such as I had never imagined.

It was nearly eight o'clock, later than usual, when I decided that it was time to wake Tante Corrie. I went to the kitchen, made a fresh pot of tea, and poured it into two china cups. Crossing the dining and living room areas, I entered the corridor leading to Tante Corrie's room. The thick curtains were still drawn and the room was dark. Entering her room I heard Tante Corrie breathing in an unusually heavy way. Not wanting to startle her from sleep, I placed the teatray as quietly as I could on her square work table in front of the window.

"Good morning, Tante Corrie," I said, as with my right hand I pulled the cords of the drapes. In the couple of seconds it took for the light to flood into the room I thought it strange that she did not reply in her normal cheerful way. I turned 'round quickly and looked down at Tante Corrie and a feeling of shock went through me like a wave. Her face was deathly pale, her chin pressed down toward her chest at an unnatural angle, and there was an odd rattling quality to her breathing. There was an expression of distress on her face. Her blue eyes looked straight at me, but she said nothing.

I ran to her side and fell to my knees beside her. "What is the matter, Tante Corrie?" I asked, taking hold of her right hand. It was cold, limp, and unresponsive. She did not reply. "Shall we pray, Tante Corrie?" was my next question. She closed her eyes. I prayed aloud, but she made no visible or audible contribution and her eyes remained closed when I had finished. Getting to my feet I noticed that the pile of books that had been on her bedside table the night before was lying in disarray on the floor. Why had she not called me? Or could she not speak and had she tried to get my attention by pushing the books from the table? For how much of the night had she been lying in this distress?

I ran to the telephone and summoned help. Before long an ambulance arrived and as if in a dream I watched the paramedics place her on a stretcher and into the ambulance. "They won't let me come in the back with you, Tante Corrie," I told her, "but I will ride in front with the driver." No response.

While Tante Corrie was undergoing examination in the hospital emergency room, I telephoned Bill and Bettie Butler and several other friends, asking them to pray. Before long many of them had arrived at the hospital.

An internist came to tell the group of us gathered in the waiting room that Tante Corrie had had a stroke and was suffering from a condition called aphasia and from partial right-sided paralysis. The speech center in the brain was affected and she was unable to speak. He did not know whether or not she would live or, if she did, whether or not speech would return. She had been taken to intensive care and I could visit her for short periods during the day. So that was what was wrong, a stroke. Would that explain her rather depressed and distant behavior of the last few days?

As soon as I was allowed, I went into the intensive care unit and was shown by a nurse to one of several cubicles. Tante Corrie was lying on her back and it was again with shock that I took in her appearance. Her eyes were closed, her face a grayish-white. Her nightwear had been exchanged for a white hospital gown tied behind her neck with strings. A square box on her right made a soft clicking sound and blinked a green number. From an elevated bottle a clear fluid dripped into a plastic tube that was attached to a needle inserted into a vein in the front of her paralyzed hand. After checking the rate of flow of the IV, the nurse left.

I shivered. It was very cold in this intensive care unit and everything seemed unreal. I wished Tante Corrie would talk to me and tell me how she was feeling, but she did not open her eyes. I asked a few questions, but receiving no response, sat next to her bed waiting. Surely she would wake up soon and the nightmare would be over.

But she did not. Several of her friends and I took turns all through the day to sit next to an unresponsive Tante Corrie. That evening the internist told me more about her condition. A stroke occurs, he explained, because of an interruption of blood supply to the brain, probably in Tante Corrie's case because of a blocked artery. The damage had occurred in the left side of her brain where the speech center was situated and it had resulted in paralysis

BIRDVILLE
BAPTIST CHURCH
LIBRARY

on her right side. He told me that if her speech did not return quickly it was possible it would not return at all.

That could not happen to Tante Corrie, I told myself. She was one of the world's best communicators. I simply could not imagine her without speech. Or without work.

During the next days I spent a lot of time at the hospital, helped and encouraged by many friends. Sometimes she was very restless and plucked at her sheet with her good left hand. At other times, to my dismay, her attitude seemed almost angry. I talked to the internist and he explained to me that this was typical of brain damage. The reaction was beyond her control. The brain had become swollen and irritated and until the effects of the trauma subsided, I would have to accept that she was very unlike her real self. But she would not remain like this, he assured me.

The internist was right. After a few days the restless, almost angry condition subsided and she became quiet. Her condition improved enough to allow her transfer from intensive care to her own room. Movement started returning to her paralyzed right arm and leg. Although she had times when she was awake and I believed she recognized me, she still could not talk.

As soon as I had the opportunity, I talked to the speech therapist assigned to Tante Corrie. The therapist explained to me that aphasia is the loss of ability to communicate in the normal way, because of brain damage. It is not simply a question of lack of speech. Understanding is also affected, which means that not only can words not be formed, but language cannot be understood. Gestures that once made sense now do not. Because brain damage is different in every case, the level of aphasia differs. In severe cases the patient cannot speak, cannot understand well, and cannot gesture appropriately. The therapist estimated that Tante Corrie's level of aphasia was severe.

This estimation proved true in the coming days. Although a limited amount of mobility returned, allowing her to swallow, to eat small amounts, and to be transferred from her bed to a wheelchair, speech and understanding were not returning.

After three weeks Tante Corrie was allowed to return to her beloved Shalom House which her friends had filled with flowers. Her radiant expression told me she was very happy to be home again.

Now that Tante Corrie needed so much extra attention, it was no longer possible for me to be her sole full-time companion. I made contact with Lotte who gave notice at her place of work in The Netherlands and made preparations to return to the United States in a couple of months. I could not wait for her to arrive.

It was strangely quiet in Shalom House that autumn. Our days had always been full of conversation and communication. Now Tante Corrie was silent and instead of being busy with at least four projects at once, she needed help with the simplest of tasks, such as getting dressed. Objects that had once been so important to her now seemed confusing. Books, for instance. It was not only that she could not read them, she no longer seemed to understand their purpose. And her desk no longer had a purpose in her life. Passing it many times a day I almost came to regard it as an enemy. It was a constant reminder that Tante Corrie had become a different person.

My role has changed, I thought to myself, as I arranged Tante Corrie's hair one morning. When I joined her two-and-a-half years earlier it was as her helper in the ministry. Now she was not going to be able to carry on her ministry as before. She needed a nurse and I was not a nurse. There was a strong bond between us but what if this condition lasted for years? This had not been what I meant when I surrendered my life to God and told Him I would do whatever He wanted. Here I was in a companion role that had many of the characteristics of marriage. The role required commitment and the laying down of my own desires. Could I fulfill it? I knew I could not in my own strength. I was glad that I had made the decision to stay with Tante Corrie before this illness happened.

As the weeks progressed there was some improvement in Tante Corrie's understanding. She seemed to comprehend most of what I said if I stated it clearly and carefully, in Dutch. She was able to respond, often with *ja* or *nee*, but could not initiate conversation.

Gradually, I began to learn the effects of her stroke. She could neither read nor write. Her gestures were confusing. Sometimes, when I asked if she would like a certain thing to eat and received a nod in response I went to the kitchen to prepare it, only to have her refuse it when I served it. She had not meant to nod her head. She thought she had shaken her head. Her responses were also inappropriate. Once I gave her a happy piece of news regarding an old friend. Instead of smiling and nodding, she burst into tears. I found this upsetting until I realized that she was not upset. She had wanted to display happy emotion.

If I had worried that Tante Corrie would not be content without work, I need not have. There was plenty of work to do in speech therapy. Believing that there was a good chance of speech returning, the speech therapist paid several visits to Shalom House each week. The three of us sat at the dining room table and I watched the proceedings.

The therapist's favorite exercise was to lay four picture cards in front of Tante Corrie depicting, for example, a key, a dog, a ball, and a spoon. Then the therapist named one and asked her to point to it. Sometimes Tante Corrie had to work hard before she arrived at the correct card. Sometimes it was very easy. I marveled that my previously strong leader could go through such a humiliatingly infantile procedure without rebellion, because I was sure that in spite of the brain damage her basic personality was unassailed. One day I thought I saw evidence of that.

Tante Corrie was sitting at the dining room table with the speech therapist to her left. I was sitting opposite Tante Corrie and thought how nice she looked in her new pale blue dress and jacket. Because she had lost weight through her recent ordeal we had paid a visit to a local store and bought three new outfits. She had been spending time sitting in the backyard among her beloved roses, had gained a tan and really looked quite healthy.

"Point to the dog, Corrie," I heard the speech therapist say. Tante Corrie gave me a quick look before applying herself to the four pictures in front of her. It was a look I had seen before. Where was it? And then I remembered two instances. One took place in Massachusetts where she received her honorary degree. On the day of the presentation she, clothed in cap and gown, marched with many of the high officials of the college to the platform. I stood in the wings and her eyes met mine. They smiled at me and they held a secret. She was telling me that she knew honorary degrees for their own sake were not too important in the eyes of God, but she was going to receive hers with humility and gratitude and offer it back to Him.

I had seen that same secret smile in her eyes when they met mine not long ago in the garden of Shalom House. A couple brought their baby to be blessed by her. They were very young and so excited that they had come up with the idea to call their daughter "Corrie." Later Tante Corrie said to me: "It is a great honor that they have called her after me, but I would have loved her just as much if she had been called Pam." Tante Corrie always saw things so matter-of-factly.

Now she was telling me through her eyes that she understood that this was a humiliating procedure, but she was going to go through it matter-of-factly. She was matter-of-fact when she was honored, and she was matter-of-fact when she was humiliated by a stroke. It reminded me of a verse in the Bible: "I have learned the secret of being content in any and every situation." It had only been a glance, but it had communicated great strength to me. *I want to be like that,* I told myself. *I want to learn to be content whatever the circumstances.*

If I found it hard to communicate with Tante Corrie, I knew it had to be much harder for her visitors, a great many of whom continued to arrive at the house. We usually received them in the sitting room and I tried to help by asking questions on Tante Corrie's behalf. I asked the kind of thing I had often heard her ask: How is your son? Tell me about your work. How has the Lord been leading you lately? Often Tante Corrie would try to form words and the visitors would listen quizzically. And often as I accompanied them to the door at the end of their visits they asked in a whisper, "What was Corrie trying to say?" My answer usually had to be that I did not know.

I began to see that it was going to be very important that I never put words in Tante Corrie's mouth, especially if other people asked me what she was trying to say. I did not know what she was thinking. Only she and God knew that. I thought I knew her well enough to be able to interpret some of her feelings and desires but I could never be her spokeswoman. And neither could anybody else.

But then I was struck with a new thought. It was true that I could not tell what she was thinking. But I could tell the effect that this extraordinary new phase in her life was having on me and on my own ministry. I could tell people about Tante Corrie's patience and consistent lack of rebellion. I could tell them how her daily surrendered attitude resulted in peace and how the peace found its way to my heart, too. Part of this new ministry I had been given must be for the sake of the visitors. When I prayed months before that the Lord make me a more godly woman, He again answered through Corrie ten Boom and, again, the key lay in maintaining an attitude of surrender.

Aphasia was a cruel affliction. I wished I could understand it better and then one day the therapist gave an example that helped me. "All of us know what aphasia is," she said. "You know how it is when you are groping for a certain word and just cannot find it. Imagine what it would be like to grope for every word and never be able to find it. That is something like Tante Corrie feels with her degree of aphasia."

I greatly missed our talks. But I was discovering that it was not necessary to have speech in order to communicate. We had lived with each other for two-and-a-half years. I knew the kinds of things that made her happy . . . watching the sunset, filling her birdfeeder and watching the birds eat, listening to Bach, walking in the neighborhood, drinking a cup of coffee outside in the sunshine. We did all those things with Tante Corrie in silence and me providing commentary now and then.

For several evenings, after Tante Corrie had gone to bed, I went through the papers in her desk, answering letters and wondering what would become of her plans for future books. One of her files was named "Book About

Betsie." She had been hoping to write a book on the life of her sister. In one of the desk drawers I found money amounting to $21 and considered adding it to the housekeeping purse. Money never had been important to Tante Corrie and now it did not mean anything. She would probably never regain her knowledge of how to use it. But to remove it from her desk seemed an invasion of her privacy. I replaced it in the drawer.

A few months after the stroke came a distressing piece of news. The speech therapist told us that there had been no improvement in Tante Corrie's condition in recent months and that she recommended stopping the lessons. This was a tremendous disappointment to Tante Corrie who had obviously been hoping that one day she would be able to speak again. She wept that evening, but before night came, after we had prayed, she seemed resolved to accept it. I did not talk to her about it in the coming weeks. We carried on with the limited means of communication that we had, rejoicing when it seemed, sometimes, that more understanding was returning.

In December 1978 we were very glad to welcome Lotte back to Shalom House. She set to work at once sorting through all Tante Corrie's writings in order to complete the daily devotional *This Day Is the Lord's*. When she found suitable pieces she read them to Tante Corrie and gained her approval—a nod, a smile, a *ja*—before committing them to type and to the publisher.

During the next months we were able to lead a fairly normal life. Having Lotte as a resident member of our household was an enormous help to me and to Tante Corrie. She had a quiet but strong personality, and was not only good at working on manuscripts but through her past work and experience knew how to run large households and to care for patients.

At the end of May 1979, as I was helping her dress one morning, Tante Corrie underwent a second stroke, losing all strength in her right side. For several days Lotte and I nursed her at home, but when it was clear that she would be more comfortable in the hospital, she was admitted there. All that Tante Corrie had gained in communicative ability was lost with her second stroke and so was the use of her right arm and leg.

When, after several weeks, Lotte and I were able to bring Tante Corrie home, we knew that we had to turn Shalom House into a little private hospital. I made arrangements for the delivery of a hospital bed, electrically automated, and a wheelchair. How glad I was that many years previously, in England, I had taken that course in basic nursing. I had not completed it and had regarded it as a failure at the time. But now I saw that my small amount of knowledge was very useful. And I also saw that even that apparent failure had been part of God's plan.

Since she was now unable to walk, we exercised Tante Corrie's limbs frequently so that she would retain as much movement as possible. We also learned how to move her from her bed to the wheelchair and she spent as much time as possible in the fresh air of her beloved back yard. There were many volunteers who helped with the yard, the cooking, sewing of special pillows for the support of her paralyzed limbs, running errands, and doing household repairs. I could see that all these people were playing their part in God's kindness to Tante Corrie at the end of her life.

But what I often thought was the end of her life turned out not to be. Successive small strokes continued to weaken her. Lotte and I were convinced, many times, that her last day had come. At such times I was often confused by remarks made by visitors or written in letters. "What a pity she has that pacemaker," said somebody. "She would have gone to heaven a long time before now if she did not have it."

"It is the good nursing care you are giving her that is keeping her alive," wrote somebody else. "If she were in a nursing home she would reach the end of this difficult road much more quickly."

While I knew that those who made the remarks meant them in kindness, not wanting her to continue to suffer, I could not help thinking that they were not looking at the whole story. Her pacemaker was the "demand" variety. It came into action only if her own heart beat below 72 per minute. And I knew from my daily readings of her pulse that it often beat above that rate, working on its own. The pacemaker could not be said to be keeping her alive. And as for putting her in a nursing home, we knew that that was not the answer. The Lord had provided all she needed in her Shalom House and we believed that she wanted to stay there.

As 1979 progressed and Tante Corrie had been ill for more than a year, I came to believe very strongly that it was not the pacemaker or good nursing care that was keeping her alive. Very often I turned for comfort to Psalm 139 and the verse that says, "All the days ordained for me were written in your book before one of them came to be." She was alive because she had not yet lived out her ordained days. God could have taken her at any one of the very low points in her illness, but her time had not yet come. God knew when that time was because He had appointed it, just as in His extraordinary plan He had appointed these circumstances in which many were playing their part. *Lord,* I often prayed, *I am so thankful that You know exactly how long this trial must last. I wish I knew. When will her time come?*

Sometimes when the days seemed endless and the skies very gray, I found myself repeating to her the very slogans I had heard Tante Corrie use in her talks.

One day she was lying on her back dressed in her beige gown. The rails of the electric bed were in their half-raised position so that Lotte and I could lean against them for extra support when we lifted her to turn her. We were all tired and for Tante Corrie it had been a day of discomfort and physical restlessness.

"Tante Corrie," I ventured, feeling I had little right to say it, "There is no pit so deep the love of God is not deeper still." She looked straight at me, smiled, and nodded. There was no sign of rebellion or disagreement on her face. But in her smile I thought I saw a deep wistfulness. And then there was a thoughtful expression on her face. Was she perhaps remembering Betsie?

One day in the concentration camp Corrie had said to Betsie, "Why are we in this terrible place?"

"I do not know," said Betsie in reply. "But in the blueprint of God's plan for our lives was the word *Ravensbruck*."

On God's blueprint for Tante Corrie's life there was also the word *stroke*. In the autumn of 1980 came a third severe episode from which Tante Corrie emerged several weeks later extremely thin and weak. This time the stroke had so debilitated her that she was not able to leave her bed. Her need for constant physical care intensified, and she also needed unbroken company. Lotte and I and two new night nurses made sure that she was never alone for more than a few minutes.

The time for all of us, including Tante Corrie I am sure, seemed to move on slowly and without the strong sense of direction we were accustomed to. In fact, however, unrecognized by me at the time, were the beginnings of the next step in my long experiment in yielding my future to God's love.

Charles and Dorothy Shellenberger from Waco, Texas, kept in touch regularly. They wrote, sent gifts, telephoned, visited Tante Corrie at Shalom House, and told me that when my task was completed they would like me to come and spend a long vacation with them in Texas.

In the early summer of 1982 came a new and deep trial. My mother wrote from England that she was entering the hospital for the investigation of small lumps under her arm. She urged me not to worry, saying that she thought it was nothing serious. But about a week later came the laboratory report that cancerous tissue had been found. My immediate desire was to fly to England, but she told me on the telephone that I should not, explaining that she had been prescribed several weeks of radiotherapy and there was no need for me to be present. She assured me that she was feeling fine.

It had been my own decision during the past years not to leave Tante Corrie for any great length of time. Board members and friends often encouraged me to take a break but I did not want to leave Tante Corrie. Now I felt torn between her and my mother. One day, a friend, knowing how I felt, sent me a quotation by Martin Luther:

"I have held many things in my hands, and I have lost them all; but whatever I have placed in God's hands, that I still possess."

My friend said in her note, "Can you put your dear mother in God's hands?"

It was one of the hardest surrenders of my life, but I did put Mother into God's hands. I remembered how once before I had been in England when she needed me at the time of her brother's death. If ever she needed me in the future I believed that God would have me at her side at the right moment. As for now, my place was with Tante Corrie.

In the winter of 1983 I sat beside Tante Corrie's bed one day while Lotte prepared tea in the kitchen. The pink hue thrown onto her skin by her deep pink nightgown gave her pale skin a healthier look than it probably rightfully had. Her hair was drawn up softly to the top of her head. Her eyes were as blue as ever. She was very thin and the well-shaped fingers below the pink lace ruffles looked particularly long. I often looked at her hands. They had done so much good in years past. They had been lifted in praise to God. They had written books and thousands of letters, played the piano and organ, won and lost chess games, and shaken the hands of rulers of state and of prisoners. Now they could not work as they used to. They were apparently doing nothing.

Then I remembered how she had often quoted to me one of her father's sayings: "A person must also be able to do nothing." I repeated it to her and she smiled and nodded.

As we waited for Lotte to bring the tea, I thought about the statement. Doing nothing, if the will of God required it, was surely a greater art for an active gifted person than was doing much. And yet she was doing it. I was watching her undergo the test. At my interview when it was first decided I should join her she had told me, "The work comes first," and I had seen how she loved her work.

For the last nearly five years there had been no work in the normal sense of the word, but in her spirit I believed there was as much work going on as there ever had been. There was a daily work of faith that God knew what He was doing with her life. And I believed I could see the results of that faith because joy and peace were present always.

I suddenly felt very rich. I had witnessed a person at the height of the opportunities of her working life. And I had seen the same person come to the place of doing no work as it was normally viewed. I resolved to try to see this time of my life when I was apparently standing still as a lesson from God in the ability to do nothing. If Tante Corrie could learn it, so could I.

March 1983, the fifth year of Tante Corrie's illness, found me looking forward to a visit from my parents. I was particularly wanting to see for myself the state of Mother's health. She had written each week and had assured me that she had had no ill effects from her radiotherapy. I decided that before they came I would do a little spring cleaning in Shalom House and one of the tasks I set myself was to tidy Tante Corrie's desk in the living room. She had not used it since 1978, and except for the work Lotte had done the files had been left basically untouched. Time had stood still for her in a way. And yet it had not. She had had other work to do and she had been obedient. Opening the drawer I again noticed the $21 in cash, which she had placed there before she first became ill and which I had not wanted to touch. Now, unexpectedly, I felt that it could be moved and put it into the household grocery purse.

At the end of March my parents arrived. Mother seemed to be doing well although she was having pain in her left leg and had difficulty walking. During their stay, Tante Corrie's condition worsened steadily. She slept for a great deal of the time and ate and drank little. We turned her often, talking to her and praying with her, but we were not sure she could hear or understand.

My mother did her share of watching and waiting at the bedside. And she did a lot more. Because of her lifetime's experience in nursing she made many good suggestions about how we might make Tante Corrie more comfortable. I was amazed at God's timing. When I had arranged for my parents to come that spring I had not known it would be at the lowest point that Tante Corrie had yet reached. Dad helped too when, in order to cause the least amount of discomfort, four of us lifted Tante Corrie when changing her position.

Tante Corrie did not have much longer to wait. About two weeks after my parents' arrival, late one evening, the night nurse summoned Lotte and me to Tante Corrie's dimly lit room. We arrived just in time to see Tante Corrie draw her last breath and leave us very quietly. For years I had wondered when her time would come. Now I knew. It was Friday, April 15, 1983, at eleven o'clock in the evening. Her ninety-first birthday. I had been with her exactly seven years.

Chapter Ten

A New Work

The days following the death of Corrie ten Boom were filled with activity. Funeral arrangements, telephone calls, letters. Mother and Dad had to meet travel commitments and I put them on a plane promising that I would see them in England as soon as possible. All at once I was aware of a deep tiredness. Although after seven years it was now possible to make plans, I did not want to. All I could think of was how good it would be to be in England. I would simply go home and rest for as long as it took to be rid of the fatigue I was feeling. There would be no commitments, nothing to do but enjoy my family and let the bracing air from the English Channel refresh and renew me. I could hardly wait.

But before I could see England again I knew there was much to be accomplished. First, Lotte and I made a point of taking leave of Tante Corrie. It had not been possible on the night she died. On our notification to them of her death, representatives of the funeral home had come at once to collect her body. Matter-of-factly they had removed from Shalom House the one around whom the life of the household had so intensely revolved. Never before had I been present at anybody's death or wanted to view a body, but now it was important to me to see her once more before her burial.

A few days after Tante Corrie's death, Lotte and I drove to the mortuary of Fairhaven Memorial Park in Santa Ana and the funeral director led us to Room B. At the back of this small and dimly lit chamber was a pale blue coffin in which lay our Tante Corrie dressed in a favorite blue nightgown and robe. Lotte was carrying a small spray of flowers. We knew that there would be many large ones at the funeral, but we wanted to give ours in private and had chosen a small arrangement in pink and yellow. The funeral director took the bouquet and placed it in her arms.

My eyes fixed on Tante Corrie's face and it was with surprise and joy that I took in her expression. Gone were the effects of the pain and difficulty at the end of her life. All the lines seemed to have fallen away and she looked beautiful. There was a nobility and a peace and the hint of a smile. *Tante Corrie*, I said to myself, *for years you could not speak and I tried not to put words in your mouth. But if I had to find words for the expression on your face now it would not be hard. You look as if you are saying, "Child, it was all worth it."*

After a few moments the funeral director closed the coffin and Lotte and I left the room. Our last goodbye had been said.

After the funeral we tackled the closing of Shalom House, my home for more than six years. There was no need to work in great haste for the Board had allowed a three-month closing period, during which Lotte and I took a three-week vacation. I was disappointed that it did not seem to help my deep weariness, but I looked forward to being in England. I knew that I could recuperate there.

The Board also suggested that I take from Shalom House any items that might be useful in furnishing my own home one day. I was grateful for this and took advantage of the offer, putting furniture in storage until an unknown date when I might have my own home.

In some ways I envied Lotte. She was returning to her apartment in The Netherlands and did not have to worry about living arrangements and future plans. She was now in her seventies and I was glad that she could rest. Lotte returned to Holland in mid-summer and in August 1983 I boarded a jet at Los Angeles International Airport, bound for London. My difficult mission was accomplished. This was the first time in nearly six years that I was going to England. During that time the Lord had helped me, greatly supported by many others, to fulfill the privilege of accompanying Tante Corrie to the end of her life.

I remembered how I had not wanted to join her in the first place, had not seen myself as the companion type, and had not wanted to commit myself wholly to her and her ministry. But I had obeyed the Lord when He asked me to go with her and had found myself not only being a companion, but coming into a very deep relationship with a woman who lived more closely to God than anybody I had ever met. And then had come those mysterious five years during which she could not talk, but still lived out all that she had ever taught me and thousands of others.

As the plane lowered toward London, giving me glimpses of emerald meadows through the clouds, my excitement mounted. My parents would be waiting for me as they had been on countless other occasions. I was coming home to stay for the first time in seventeen years, and for the first several weeks I was going to sleep.

Sure enough, Mother and Dad were waiting for me at the airport, but it was with shock that I saw Mother seated in a wheelchair. I knew that her left leg had been painful but did not realize that she now had this degree of immobility. After we had greeted each other and had settled in the car, Dad began the two-hour journey through the Sussex countryside to Hastings. On the way Mother explained that a bone disease had recently been diagnosed and that the correct treatment was being sought. My heart began to sink. Was it possible that having been through a painful illness with Tante Corrie I was now going to have to witness illness in my mother?

When we arrived at their little house on the cliffs overlooking the Channel (of which my parents had been the sole occupants since the death of my grandmother several years earlier) it did not take long to see that Mother's painful leg was incapacitating her severely. She received me into their home with her usual loving hospitality, however, even struggling upstairs because she wanted to see my face when I viewed the front bedroom she and Dad had had newly decorated for me. I admired the new carpeting and the fresh wallpaper with its green and white pattern offset with white paintwork, but the thing to which my eye was mainly drawn was a rectangular card propped up on the mantlepiece. Eleven words were written in varying shades of green and in the top lefthand corner was a variegated butterfly, colored with a child's hand. It was a card of welcome for me from little Naomi, Sylvia's nine-year-old daughter. The words were from Psalm 143: "Teach me to do your will, for you are my God."

That night as I lay in bed, a bluish light from the streetlamps allowed me to make out those eleven words dimly. I read and reread them and it was as if the Lord asked me to make another surrender of my will to Him, based on the words *For You are my God.*

I reviewed the main touchpoints in the past eighteen years since I had first trusted God. My fear that He might want me to leave England had come to pass. But looking back I would not have missed what He gave me instead. I had been afraid to speak in public but the past years had proved that I could not only do it with the Lord's help, but had learned to enjoy it very much. I had been afraid to be single for the Lord's sake, but look what I had gained instead. He had allowed me to help one of His servants whom He had used greatly and to be at her side in her death. How could I have done that had I married? He had proved to me that He was my God. I knew Him personally. He was doing what was best for me whether or not I could see it at the time.

Now after years of hard work I very much wanted rest, but I had seen from my mother's condition that she might need nursing care soon.

God was again asking me to make a new, deeper surrender to Him. I was not asked to pray, "Teach me to do Your will, for You will then give me the desires of my heart." Or, ". . . for then I will have a clear conscience." I was asked to pray, "Teach me to do Your will, for You are my God." There were to be no conditions attached.

In the front room of the little house on the cliff with the bluish streetlamps lighting the eleven words on the card on the mantlepiece and the sound of the waves beating against the beach, God gave me the grace to make one more unconditional surrender to Him.

After I had been in England three days, Mother had to take to her bed and I found myself applying to her nursing care many of the things I had learned at Tante Corrie's bedside. I could not get over the timing of my being with her. Years before I had been in this little house when Mother received a telephone call that her brother had died. It was remarkable that I should be in England just then, and the only one of her children at home. At that time the coinciding of the events encouraged me to believe that if I was ever needed in England I would be in the right place at the right time. Now I was seeing the reward of that faith. God in His kindness had brought me to Mother's side just when I needed her and she needed me, not too soon and not too late.

We spent many hours together in her upstairs bedroom overlooking the bay. At 67, Mother hardly had a gray hair and her smooth complexion would have been the envy of many women twenty years younger. In her voice, which sounded like a song, she told me about her childhood in Wales, her nurses' training in London during the war, and how she and Dad met and married and moved to Hastings. And there were many stories from her long nursing career. One day as I was busying myself getting Mother prepared for the day I caught her looking at me with evident pride.

"You have changed," she said.

"How?" I asked her.

"Well," she replied, "you have become more confident and more willing to help others in a practical way. I did not tell you, but when Dad and I first visited Shalom House Tante Corrie told me that she wanted you to learn to see things in the right proportions. She set out to change you, and she did."

Inside, I rejoiced that there was a change in me and that it was obvious to my mother. What extraordinary means God had used to bring about the change! Seven years spent in the company of a woman more than fifty years my senior and nearly five of those years in the role of companion and nurse.

What other changes needed to take place in me, I wondered? What could I learn while we waited for Mother to regain her health?

During my years with Tante Corrie I had learned to conceal my own sorrow, I believed, for the sake of our patient. Sometimes if I sensed that a visitor was likely to become emotional, even to the point of shedding tears at Tante Corrie's noncommunicative condition, I warned them that tears could upset our patient and that if they had to cry they should wait until they were no longer in her presence. Mother had watched this stiff-upper-lip attitude in me.

"Don't ever be hardhearted, Pammy," she said to me now. "Let people be sorrowful, for they are helped not only when you share joys with them, but also when you share their grief."

She went on to give me an example from her nursing experience of several years before. A young girl had been drowned in the Channel and it was Mother's task to accompany her parents to the hospital morgue for the identification of their daughter's body.

"I don't know who cried harder," said Mother, "me or the parents. But afterward the child's mother took me aside and told me how much my sharing of her grief had helped her bear her sorrow. Be careful that you learn how to enter into people's sorrows."

I decided to make a firm note of that piece of advice. Perhaps my being with Mother in this inactive part of her life was to learn from her rich store of wisdom.

The coming weeks saw many visits to hospitals for further tests as Mother's condition deteriorated. In November, the news we had feared was finally diagnosed. Although its presence had been masked by a bone disease, the real culprit was cancer. We were informed that it had spread throughout her body and that no cure was possible.

The end of that month saw my fortieth birthday. Mother was moved to a private hospital room and to my grief I learned that the cancer had caused secondary growths in her brain. Her lovely outgoing personality was muted and she could not communicate as before. But I thanked God that having been through something similar with Tante Corrie I could recognize brain damage for what it was and know that Mother's spirit, safe in the hands of the Lord Jesus, was unassailable. Just before Christmas, eight months after Tante Corrie's homegoing, late one evening when Dad, Sylvia, Digger, and I were gathered 'round her bed, the Lord took Mother.

After the funeral, Dad and I traveled north with Sylvia, Bruce, and their family to spend Christmas and the beginning of the New Year at their home near Manchester in the north of England. The welcome we received from Bruce's church did much to comfort us in our loss. Dad began to encourage me to think about future plans, urging me to step out again and not to stay in England.

During the months of Mother's illness I had accepted several invitations to speak about what I learned during the last years of Tante Corrie's life. I tried to explain that although it would not appear that Tante Corrie's life was very useful, paralyzed and speechless as she was, God had shown me that she was extremely valuable in His sight. I could see that the message was helping people. "Why don't you write down some of these things you have learned?" several asked me. The suggestion had even come from John and Elizabeth Sherrill. At first I had dismissed the idea. How ever could I write a book? But the question kept returning to my mind.

During my stay with Sylvia I received several requests to join various ministries but none aroused a sense of anticipation in me. One day, however, I received a telephone call from a young American woman who was part of the advance team of the Billy Graham Association. I had met Glenda six years previously in Sweden and she had kept in touch. Now in England, she told me that her next assignment was Anaheim, California, where a Crusade was to be held in the summer of 1985. Glenda suggested that I consider being part of the local staff in Anaheim. I made a note of her telephone number but knew that I was too tired even to consider such a proposal right now. Far more appealing was an invitation from Charles and Dorothy Shellenberger to visit them in Texas "just for a time of quiet." I accepted immediately and planned to make the trip after spending some time with Sylvia's family.

One evening when the four children were in bed and Bruce was at a church meeting, Sylvia and I sat at her dining room table, our hands cupped around mugs of hot chocolate. It was cold and raw outside and a bitter wind swept across those "Wuthering Heights" moors. I had become part of the household during the past weeks but knew the time was coming when once again we would have to part.

"Perhaps, Pammy," said my sister unexpectedly, looking at me with her serious gray eyes, "the time has come for you to marry."

I decided to take up her theme and to dream a little. "Maybe I'll meet the man of my dreams when I arrive in Texas."

"Why Texas, of all places?" asked my sister, sipping her hot chocolate.

"I like Texans. Nearly all of them are tall and friendly. And," I added facetiously, "a lot of them are rich. Perhaps I could meet somebody who would take care of me and help your ministry, too.

"But marriage is just a dream, Sylvia," I added, serious now. "I do not think there is anybody who would be suitable. I have worked in so many places and I'd want to marry somebody with similar experience. I have been through some very unusual and mysterious years. Could there ever be anybody who could understand that?"

But there was an even greater hurdle. As the wind howled across the moors outside the dining room window I remembered the evening I had spent in California with a man who I discovered had been divorced. "Now that I am forty years old," I told Sylvia, "it's unlikely that I could meet anybody who has not been married before. He would have to be a widower. I would not marry anybody who has been divorced."

I expected Sylvia to nod her agreement and was surprised at the answer I received.

"Why is it not possible that the Lord could have such a marriage for you?" she said. "Through our work Bruce and I have met Christians who are divorced—often against their will. As we worked with them we've learned more about how merciful God is."

Sylvia had a way of shocking me and she had just done so again. Sylvia, staunchly evangelical, basing her whole life on biblical principles, had apparently found that, at times, the working out of those principles was very complex and was much harder than people often thought.

The voice of her younger twin, calling from his bedroom at the end of the corridor, interrupted our conversation. Sylvia left and I was alone at the table, very thoughtful. Who was I that I should put everyone who had been divorced into a group and label them as wrong? Divorce itself was wrong, but what—as Sylvia had pointed out—of the people who had been forced into divorce against their will?

Shortly after that conversation I took leave of Sylvia and her family and traveled back to the south coast so that Dad and I could spend some weeks together before I left. It was hard to think of leaving him alone, but he was adamant that I make plans for my future. He decided that he would make another visit to America shortly to visit a close family friend whose husband had recently died. The knowledge that we would meet up again in Los Angeles in mid-April made my departure easier and in the last week of February I boarded a plane for Waco, Texas, where I was met by Charles and Dorothy Shellenberger. They drove me to their comfortable home, familiar from my stay there with Tante Corrie nearly eight years earlier, and installed me in a large room that was to be mine for a whole month.

Dorothy explained that this was a room where Christian workers could rest. It was called the "Elisha Room," taking its name from the story in 2 Kings 4 in which a man and woman prepare a room where the prophet Elisha could rest every time he passed their way. I could not wait to get unpacked.

Waco seemed to have changed little from my last visit. Situated on the flatlands of central Texas, surrounded by farming country, it had a population of just over one hundred thousand and the wide expanse of the sky still reminded me of The Netherlands. The air was fresh and clean and the people very friendly. They spoke slowly with a long flat sound to the "a" vowel. As the days passed I began to unwind inside.

I did need to do one piece of work while I was in Waco. On my way from England I had made contact with Chosen Books, whose co-founders John and Elizabeth Sherrill had encouraged me to write a book about Corrie ten Boom's final years. Stopping over at their headquarters in Lincoln, Virginia, I asked if they would still be interested in such a book and received a positive reply. I had come to Waco now, having determined that I would write an outline for a proposed book and submit it to them for comment.

One afternoon alone in the Elisha Room I sat at a small table and prayed that God would give me an outline for a book. I had had no formal training in writing and all I could go on was the suggestions the editors at Chosen Books had given me . . . that I write a brief synopsis of the material I thought should be in the book, divided into several chapters.

Praying that God would guide me, I made a mental journey through the seven years of my work with Tante Corrie, isolated some main points, illustrated them with examples and sent the outline to Virginia under the title *The Five Silent Years.* Chosen Books wrote back that they would be interested in my developing the material along the lines I had presented. On receipt of their letter I discovered that something in me very much wanted to take up the challenge of trying to write down some of the vital things Tante Corrie's illness had taught me. Perhaps it could help many people. I noticed a real sense of looking forward to a project.

Waco's March weather was sunny and warm and while Charles worked at his pediatric clinic, Dorothy and I took long daily walks. I told her that I had little idea of what the future held except that I was trying to write a book.

"We would like it very much if you would come and live here in Waco," Dorothy said one morning as we took a walk in the sun.

"When Corrie and you were here before," she went on, "I asked Corrie to return. She said that her traveling days were over but I remember you mouthed the words 'I'll be back' to me. And here you are."

"I love Waco," I replied, "but I really do not know what

kind of work I could do. Waco is right off the beaten track."

"Perhaps there is a husband for you in Texas," Dorothy said, unexpectedly.

I laughed and told her that my sister and I had had a similar conversation, but that I could not imagine meeting anybody suitable. I told her that years ago, when I worked for Brother Andrew in Holland, the Lord asked me to stop praying for a husband. "But perhaps through you and Sylvia He is saying that I should begin to pray again."

"What kind of husband would you want?" said Dorothy, apparently not wanting to leave the subject yet. "I have just read a true story about a woman who made a list of the qualities she wanted in a husband. She presented the list to God and some time later met and married a man very like the one described on her list."

I had to admit that I did not have a list. I didn't even know what I would put down on such a list except that a possible future husband would need to identify with the unusual life I had lived up until now.

Dorothy and I returned to the house for lunch, but our conversation stayed with me through the afternoon. Was it time now to begin praying again for a husband? Alone in the Elisha Room I did a lot of thinking. I had never regretted laying in the Lord's hands my right to marriage. But now both Sylvia and Dorothy, two women who prayed for me regularly, had brought up the subject. I got on my knees.

"Lord," I prayed, "I do not know Your future will for me. But if it is in Your will, please give me a good and godly man."

Later that day Dorothy and Charles and I attended the Wednesday evening service of their home church, Highland Baptist Church in Waco. Midway through the service, a soloist was invited to the podium. She seemed to be

directing her words straight at me. It was a song I had
never heard before: "Your Maker is your husband; the
Lord of hosts is His name." The words came from the
book of the prophet Isaiah and to me they confirmed my
original direction from the Lord that I was not to pray for
a husband. "Your Maker is your husband. . . ." I did not
need more. And indeed up until now God had provided
all that I needed.

Furthermore, that night in the Elisha Room, I took out
my battered copy of *Daily Light*, a devotional guide in
which groups of Scripture verses are arranged in morning
and evening readings. Each section has its own theme.
When I opened my copy with its worn burgundy cover
that night my eye fell on these words: "Your Maker is your
husband; the Lord of hosts is his name. . . ."

What a coincidence! The other selections on the same
theme went on: "You shall no more be termed Forsaken
. . . for the Lord delighteth in you. As the bridegroom
rejoices over the bride, so shall your God rejoice over you.
I will greatly rejoice in the Lord . . . for he has clothed me
with the garments of salvation, . . . as a bride adorns herself with jewels. I will betroth you to me for ever; yes, I will
betroth you to me in righteousness."

Although I knew that those words were in general
meant for the whole Church, I read them against the
background of my prayer of that morning that God would
give me a husband. There was no doubt in my mind now.
Coupled with the song in church just this evening on the
same theme, I knew that God was telling me this: now
was not the time for Him to answer my prayer. He was
asking me to step out into an unknown future trusting
Him.

Chapter Eleven

A Specific Prayer

After a month's vacation I left Waco, not only refreshed but also with something accomplished. I had written the outline for a book and had received encouragement from all sides to write down what I had learned from Tante Corrie's years of illness.

It was therefore with a growing sense of urgency to get down to work that I headed once again for California, in mid-April. I had contacted my friend Arlene, one of Tante Corrie's housekeepers, who had invited me to stay with her and her little daughter, Amy, if I should come back to Placentia. I wrote that I would be glad to accept.

In Los Angeles, on the way, I met up with my father, who arrived in California from England at about the same time as I. Little did I suspect that I was about to receive the biggest surprise of my life so far. Dad had come to visit that family friend, a widow who had moved to Southern California. I liked and admired Irene but was totally unprepared when Dad told me they had become engaged and would like to be married the next month. He and Irene had both had exceptionally happy marriages and were paying their spouses a high compliment in wanting to remarry so soon. Marriage for them had been so good that life was not complete without it.

After the surprise, I also had feelings of relief that Dad would not be facing the future alone. Was God also preparing a way for me in this decision of Dad's to remarry? Suddenly, for the first time in my adult life, I found that no one depended on me for help. What a strange feeling! After surrendering all of my rights, including the "right" to my own marriage, I had become the Lord's responsibility. What would He do next?

Leaving Dad and Irene, then, to pursue their plans, I took off for Placentia. Arlene and little Amy made me welcome. My room, with beige carpeting and wooden shutters, was at the front of the house and just large enough for a single bed, a small easy chair, a bookcase— and a typewriter.

It was good to be back in Placentia where I had spent six years with Tante Corrie. As I settled down once again I often thought about Shalom House, just fifteen minutes' walk from where I was now living. It had been rental property and when we moved out had reverted to its owners who had sold it. Wanting to meet the new owners and tell them something about what had happened in their home in previous years, I knocked on the door on several occasions. Never could I find anybody home. Deciding that when I had closed the door of Shalom House for the last time I had also closed that chapter of my life, I made no more attempts to visit our old home.

It was time to focus my attention on the proposed book, but I also had to ask myself whether such a project was practical. Although Tante Corrie's Board had paid me a salary for six months after I left their service, I now had no income. How was I to support myself during the months it might take to write a book? I had a sum of money in my savings account but knew that I could not live on it for long.

One day I received an unexpected offer from a friend. He asked me to make a list of my anticipated expenses for the coming months and then to let him know the result because he wanted to help meet those expenses with a monthly check. I was touched and astonished. Nothing like it had ever happened to me. Drawing up a list of basic expenses, I mailed it to my friend who soon sent me a check to cover the whole list. And he promised to do the same during each of the months I was writing the book. I accepted his generous offer, believing that God was using him to help provide for me. My thoughts went back to my conclusion in Waco that God at this time was not going to answer my prayers for a husband. "Your Maker is your husband" were the words with which He had impressed me so strongly. And now I was seeing my Maker's provision for me through His servants.

He even provided me with a place to write. One day I paid a visit in nearby Fullerton to Mrs. Elfstrom whose husband, until his recent death, had been a Board member. When I told Mrs. Elfstrom about my plan to write a book she offered me the use of her cabaña, a self-contained, private, and quiet room separate from her main house. I accepted her offer gratefully and soon began the task of writing.

It was good to return each evening to Arlene and eight-year-old Amy's home. Over dinner each night we shared the events of our respective days. After Amy had gone to bed, Arlene and I often sat in the living room with a cup of tea. A frequent discussion was the question of divorce. Arlene's husband had left her two years earlier and he had still not filed for divorce. She did not believe it was right for her to take steps to bring a legal end to the marriage, but I could see that she was in an extremely difficult situation. Was she married? As far as I could see there was no real marriage and had not been for years. This was the first time I had been this close to a separated couple and over our evening cups of tea I listened as Arlene opened her heart to me. What was she to do?

I tried to identify with her in her grief and recalled one of my last conversations with my sister in England. Through her I had seen that my attitude of lumping all separation victims together and labeling them as wrong was unmerciful. I had resolved to allow God to help me see from His point of view some of the griefs of those who had been separated and divorced. And here I was with Arlene in her grief at her own unfathomable future.

I decided to spend some time finding out what the Bible has to say on divorce and remarriage. In my little room I read many of the passages in the Bible having to do with marriage. They underlined what I already knew. Marriage was intended to be for life. Nothing should dissolve it. But I thought about Arlene's situation and knew that her husband, an unbeliever, had left her. The marriage *had* been dissolved against her will. In her case was it only a legal contract that bound her? And should that bind her for life if her husband was set on not returning? I came to believe not.

I continued my daily work in the cabaña at Mrs. Elfstrom's home, trying to write twenty pages per chapter. The Scripture that seemed to dominate my thoughts was from Psalm 31, which I had heard Tante Corrie quote often: "My times are in Your hands."

In my mind as I wrote I saw a panorama of Tante Corrie's life and how she had learned to accept the difficult things that happened to her as allowed by God. "All our times are in His hands, child," she had often said to me, "even the difficult ones." With that Scripture verse in mind I applied myself to writing. And to reminding myself that this time in my life was also in God's hands.

One of the tokens of God's kindness to me that year was to have my father near. He and his new wife, Irene, spent several months in Hemet in Southern California, and I was able to visit them often.

When I was about halfway through the draft manuscript, I decided that I needed to give serious thought and prayer to finding work. Although my friend was sending money regularly to meet my expenses, I knew that it would be for a limited time. Remembering how Glenda, the friend who worked with the Billy Graham Crusade, had told me that there would be a large Southern California Crusade the next year, 1985, and that local staff would be needed, I telephoned her and asked for an appointment with the Crusade Director. Very soon it was confirmed that I was welcome to meet him to discuss the possibilities of my helping the local committee of the Billy Graham Crusade. Here again the Lord provided my exact need, for the job subsequently found was not mentally demanding and allowed me plenty of emotional space for the book.

By August 1984 I had finished the first draft of my proposed book and sent it to Chosen Books in Virginia. A few weeks later I received a very encouraging telephone call. A representative of Chosen Books told me that the company was interested in publishing *The Five Silent Years of Corrie ten Boom.* He invited me to come to Virginia to learn how to rewrite and develop the manuscript under the guidance of John Sherrill.

I considered the offer to be a great honor. Ever since I had first read books written or co-authored by John and his wife, Tibby, I had had great respect for them. Never had I put down half-finished any book of theirs.

But there was another reason why I looked forward to seeing this couple again. I wanted to thank them for the part they had had in God's guidance in my life. If it had not been for *God's Smuggler*, co-authored by them, I would not have crossed the English Channel in 1968 to help Brother Andrew in The Netherlands. I might never have come to know Corrie ten Boom with whom my life was to become so deeply bound and through whom I would learn so much. It seemed fitting to me that having had a large part in the writing of *The Hiding Place*, which told about the first part of her life, John Sherrill should be the one to direct the writing of a book describing the end of Tante Corrie's journey.

Traveling to the little town of Lincoln, Virginia, I met John and Tibby once more. It had been many years since we had last seen each other in Holland, but they had changed little. They impressed me by their interest in my project. I could tell that they had a deep love and respect for Tante Corrie and were as keen as I was that the story of the last years of her life should be told. John said that he and I would begin work tomorrow at the Chosen Books office. Tibby would be working with an author on a different project.

One evening toward the end of my week in Virginia, John and Tibby invited me to have dinner with them at a restaurant in a small town nearby. I loved what I had seen of life in this Eastern part of the country. It reminded me of England. Winding narrow roads through wooded countryside led to one small town after another. *Villages* would have been my English word for them.

The evening light had faded by the time we reached the small restaurant where John had made reservations for us.

We were led to a quiet corner and seated ourselves at a square table for four, laid with a thick, starched white tablecloth and silverware. In the center of the table a candle encased in glass threw a soft light on the two people opposite me. John was wearing a beige suit and yellow waistcoat. There was something about him that always reminded me of an Englishman. Was it the way he wore his beard? Or was it the slight inflection in his voice that betrayed the fact he had once lived in Oxford? Tibby was wearing a camel skirt and brown woollen sweater. I wondered if the color coordination in their clothes was design or coincidence. I thought that being a husband/wife writing team must hold many challenges, but surely must be one of the most interesting kinds of partnerships.

My first impression of Tibby, years before when I had helped with some typing while *The Hiding Place* was being written, was that she was a sensitive and reflective woman. That impression had been underlined this week. "Tell us more about your life *since* Corrie's death, Pam," she said as we awaited our meal.

I launched into what I hoped was an abbreviated account of the events of the past one-and-a-half years, ending with: "I sometimes wish I knew what the future held."

"I think you will probably marry," said John unexpectedly.

I smiled and told them how my sister, Sylvia, in England and my friend Dorothy in Texas had also brought up the subject.

"Dorothy even suggested that I make a list of the qualities I would like in a husband," I said, laughing.

"Well, have you?" asked Tibby quietly.

"Well, no," I replied. "I just cannot imagine the kind of man who would be suitable for me. But seeing this is the third time it has come up, let me see if I can name a few things I would really appreciate having in a husband. First of all, he must love God and want to serve Him, but apart from that I would like to have a husband who is gentle and compassionate and who has an interest in writing. And I would also like him to be good-looking."

"Let us pray for that together before the evening ends," said John.

And we did. John and Tibby took my list of desired qualities in a husband so seriously that they prayed according to the description I had made. And they undertook to pray in the future too. For the third time I had been challenged to be specific regarding qualities in a future husband. I went to bed thoughtfully that night.

My week of learning in Virginia was over. It was time to head back to California and begin rewriting my book. It was not until much later that I remembered the prayer.

The busy months passed quickly as I reworked my manuscript. My roommate, Arlene, began nurses' training. It was necessary for her now to receive schooling that would ensure her and Amy of a better income, for she had received notice of divorce proceedings from her husband's lawyer, raising still again for us discussions about God's love for men and women whose marriages had been dissolved.

Finally the day came when I mailed my rewritten manuscript off to Chosen Books and made plans for a visit to England. After resting there I expected to return to the United States to undertake speaking engagements at the time of the publication of my book early the next year, 1986.

My publisher had requested I help make the book known by accepting speaking appointments. I would therefore try to speak as often as I could. My Texan friends, the Shellenbergers, had invited me to come back to Waco to spend some time with them and speak at their church. Waco would be my first official speaking engagement.

In the first week of January 1986, I awoke with a most unusual sense of adventure and excitement. Was the Lord underlining that something significant was going to happen on this new journey to the States?

Chapter Twelve

Decisions

Dr. and Mrs. Shellenberger were waiting for me when I arrived at the airport of Texas's capital city, Austin. By now they had met so many of my planes that it was almost like coming home to my parents. It was nearly ten years since we had first met and they still made a very handsome couple, Charles with his sandy hair and engaging smile and white-haired Dorothy with her beautiful brown eyes.

Sooner than I could have wished, it was time to prepare for the evening meeting at Charles and Dorothy's church, Highland Baptist. I decided to wear a green knit suit with a pleated skirt and straight jacket offset with gold buttons. As I viewed myself in the mirror in my room, however, I noticed that the suit had a tighter fit than usual. I must have gained weight during my vacation. I also took a critical look at my hair. Just before leaving England I had had it cut and the hairdresser had trimmed it rather too short. None of the permanent was left and my hair looked perfectly straight, short, and flat. I tried to arrange it so that the gray hairs, which had been showing themselves in increasing numbers lately, would not be too obvious.

So far my appearance was not pleasing to me. Next I studied my face. As a result of England's cold winter winds, it had a dry appearance. I tried to camouflage this by adding an extra layer of moisturizer before putting on my makeup, but the mirror did not reveal much improvement. Never had I been so displeased at my appearance when preparing to speak.

Just before 7 P.M. Charles, Dorothy, and I arrived at Highland Baptist Church and made our way to a row of seats on the left side of the semi-circular church. My mind went back two years to the day when I'd asked God to give me a good and godly husband. It was just a few hours later in this same church, in 1984, when the soloist sang, "Your Maker is your husband; the Lord of hosts is His name." And that same night, having read those identical words from Isaiah 54 in my devotional book, I concluded that the message I had heard at Highland Baptist Church was God's guidance for me at that time. He, the Lord, was my husband. He would take care of me. And He had. Right up until now, Sunday, January 19, 1986.

The evening service started with songs of praise and then it was my turn to take the microphone. Silently I prayed that God would use this time to help people in the congregation. Then I traced the years of Tante Corrie's illness and gave examples of how truly her times had been in God's hands. There was a hush over the congregation and I could sense God's presence strongly. On reaching the end of my talk, I rejoined the Shellenbergers at the left of the church. There was prayer and more singing and the service ended.

As we prepared to leave our pew, I saw that several people from this friendly crowd of Texans were making their way toward us. One by one, college student, mother, businessman, they shook my hand or hugged me and told how the message had helped them.

Suddenly Charles Shellenberger was standing in front of me saying, "Pam, this is Carey Moore. He would like to be introduced to you."

I looked up into the eyes of a tall, slender, and good-looking man in his early fifties, about ten years older than I. His lean face had a certain wistful quality to it. Just behind him was a young man in his late teens whose face was very similar.

"Hello, Pam," said this Mr. Carey Moore. We shook hands and he introduced me to his son, Jim.

"I like your accent," was Carey's next remark.

"You are the one with the accent," I replied. We both laughed.

"I was very interested in your message and in what you had to say about Eastern Europe," he said. "I visited there last year. Also, your having written a book interests me. I am an editor with Word Books here in Waco." After this brief introduction, Carey asked if perhaps we might have a meal together in the next week to see what friends and acquaintances we might have in common.

After I had given him my hosts' telephone number, Carey and I took leave of each other and I made my way home with Charles and Dorothy. When bedtime came, I closed my eyes and made a mental recapitulation of the events of the past few hours. For some reason my mind dwelt on my memory of the kind face of the editor from Word Books. I had met his son, but where was Carey's wife? And why did he seem familiar?

Carey Moore phoned the next day and during the call he left no doubt about his marital status. "I have been through an unfortunate divorce," he told me. Immediately I recalled Sylvia's advice that I show more concern for the suffering of divorced people. I wondered anyway why Carey was showing interest in me and knew it could not have much to do with the way I had looked last evening with my ill-fitting suit and straight hair and dried-out skin. He must have been particularly interested in what I had said about Eastern Europe. We arranged to have supper together on Friday evening. For some reason I looked forward to seeing him again.

Arriving at the Shellenbergers' early on Friday evening, Carey suggested having supper in a cafeteria at one of Waco's shopping malls. There was a cinema in the mall, he explained, and it was showing a movie he thought I might enjoy. We could decide on that later.

About half-an-hour later, we were seated opposite each other in the quietest corner of the restaurant. I took in Carey's appearance with more attention than I had been able to give Sunday after church. His mid-brown hair was graying, his eyes were hazel. He wore gray pants and a navy blazer. His face was particularly kind, but it certainly held a sort of wistful sadness.

After we had exchanged some general conversation, Carey told me that he was glad he had gone to Highland Baptist Church last Sunday night because he had liked the message I had given.

"I moved to Waco only last September," he repeated, "when Word Books invited me to become editor for their academic books. Before that I had lived for nine years in New Jersey."

"And your son Jim?" I asked. "He lives here, too?"

"Yes. Jim has a job as a waiter," replied Carey. "While he's saving money for college he is living with me in my apartment. Jim is my second son. He is nineteen. I have an older boy who is in the Navy, and two younger daughters, both in New Jersey with their mother."

Carey went on to explain that he had been separated from his family for five years. In 1984, his wife's divorce action had become final. He spoke with sadness, but without bitterness. He told me that it had been a hard decision to leave New Jersey where he had worked as an editor for Fleming H. Revell, Corrie ten Boom's publisher. For a few minutes we talked about staff members whom we both knew. Carey went on to tell me that he had prayed carefully and had sought the advice of his pastor and a few close friends before accepting the invitation to come to Waco. Although he had grown up and attended college in Texas, and moving there would be like returning home, it would mean that he would see his daughters, ages twelve and sixteen, only rarely.

We had finished our supper by now and were sipping coffee. Carey was interested in my English background and work experience of the last twenty years. And I was interested in his. His career in Christian journalism had taken him to many countries and parts of North America. We talked about his recent visit to Eastern Europe and what we had both learned from the suffering Church. And we discovered that we knew many people in common. We laughed a lot, too. Carey seemed to have a lighthearted love of life and an optimistic nature.

By now it was far too late for us to go to the movie, so after a walk, Carey took me home. Dorothy's brown eyes were full of curiosity as I went to the sitting room to say goodnight to her and Charles. I told her as casually as possible that I had enjoyed my evening. I did not want to admit even to myself that I was feeling drawn in an unusual way to my new friend. Again I wondered to myself why he seemed familiar. I was sure we had not met before.

My plan was to spend two more weeks in Waco before traveling on to California where a young woman friend acting as my agent was in the process of arranging speaking engagements for me. Dorothy had also arranged more speaking for me in Waco and the days were full. Carey continued to call every day and we met now and then—for walks, for Bible study with a small group in his apartment, and to attend a speaking engagement to which he drove me.

After a Sunday afternoon walk with Carey, I thought I'd have a word with Dorothy. I knew that she and Charles had liked Carey from the moment they met him at Highland Baptist Church, but what did she think about our meeting as often as we were?

"Do you think it is all right for me to spend time with Carey?" I asked her as the two of us were preparing supper.

"Whyever not?" was her encouraging reply. "It is a lot better than staying home watching television with two people old enough to be your parents."

One cold day at the end of January, Carey came up with an idea. He knew the hostess of a Christian radio program in Dallas that was broadcast nationally. It could be a good means of giving coverage to my book, and he would see if he could arrange to drive me there himself. I accepted his offer with thanks. And I had to admit that I was looking forward to spending a day with Carey. Never had I felt so comfortable in a man's presence. And this man knew how to treat a woman. He opened and closed doors for me, walked on the outside of pavements, and even turned on the heater of his 1979 pale blue Malibu for several minutes before seating me in it.

And if his thoughtfulness impressed me, his prayers did far more. Through them I learned more about Carey than through his conversation. He was earnest in his desire to know God, he had compassion for those in distress, and he wanted to be used to help bring others to know Jesus Christ. I prayed that this new friendship would be in the will of God. I remembered that I had always told myself that I would never marry a divorced man. But then I brought myself up short. Who was talking about marriage? All this kind man had offered was to drive me to a radio station in Dallas.

And he did. On the morning before I was to fly to California, we drove to Dallas, talking nonstop all the way. After a sandwich lunch we found the radio station and I went through an hour-long live interview, discovering to my alarm that I was expected to answer telephone inquiries from across the nation at the end of the program as part of the broadcast. Marveling that God could take someone who was once as shy as I and so change her, I found myself able to deal with a variety of questions.

At the end of the afternoon Carey took me on a short tour of the city, ending up at a Mexican restaurant, complete with mariachi band. By this time we had discovered an impressive list of the things we had in common, from a love of words and word derivations, to reading, writing, letter-writing, walking, swimming. The only area of Carey's interests where I did not feel at home was the mysterious world of American football.

By mid-evening we were on the freeway again, heading south to Waco. With a journey of a hundred miles before us, I wondered why Carey was driving so slowly. But I was glad. This gave us more time together. Tomorrow I had to leave Waco and might not see him again.

The car was warm and comfortable. I settled back in my seat feeling very contented about the day behind us. We talked now and then but when there were pauses neither of us apparently felt we had to fill them with words. I wondered if Carey felt as comfortable in my presence as I did in his.

And then came an unexpected question. "Do you believe God has called you to a single life, or would you like to marry one day?" he said, giving me a quick sideways glance.

Startled, I paused a minute before answering, then launched into an explanation. "Years ago, when I committed my life to God's service, I told Him that if He wanted me to be single for His sake I would be," I replied. "I told Him that I would never seek marriage. It was a very hard decision for me to make because I had always wanted a husband and children. Then God led me to do work I could never have done had I married and I have never regretted remaining single. But I have not committed myself to a single life. I want to do God's will whether it is to be married or to be single."

Carey drove on in silence for a short while, then said: "I would like to tell you the circumstances that led to the ending of my marriage. Do you mind?"

"No," I replied, "I would like you to."

A light rain was falling as the blue Malibu made its way to Waco. The night was very dark. Little light fell into the car but I turned toward Carey as he explained that he had married in 1962, here in Texas, and that the coming years had taken him and his wife to various parts of the United States. He had a keen desire to work in Christian journalism and the various opportunities offered him meant frequent moves for his family of four children. As time went on his relationship with his wife deteriorated.

"My failings were many," said Carey. "But the main fault was in my lack of consideration for her feelings and my stubborn determination to do 'God's work' without really waiting submissively on Him."

Much effort, including Christian counseling, was made to mend the relationship, with no improvement, and Carey's wife began to insist that he move out. This he resisted. Finally, when communication was at a low point, their Christian psychologist advised separation. Carey agreed to this in June 1981, believing it to be a temporary measure.

During the coming months he did all that he knew to do to bring about reconciliation. He mobilized friends and family to pray with him in an effort to keep his home intact. Still, after several years there came a time when he could no longer believe for reconciliation. In 1984 he and his wife were divorced.

It was with difficulty and obvious pain that Carey told his story. I had heard it in his voice and I saw it in his eyes as he ended his explanation and looked at me briefly in the dim light in the car.

"Thank you for telling me," I said.

I did not speak to him about what I was thinking, for I was not sure myself. Many things were going through my mind. I was mainly struck by the fact that Carey had ascribed no blame to his ex-wife and there was no bitterness in his references to her. There was obvious grief at his failure and sorrow for the effects on the family. I was very sorry, too, but I felt no pity for Carey. Here was a man who had gone through a very deep valley, but who had repented of his mistakes and found that God had forgiven him.

By now we had arrived at Waco and Carey delivered me to the Shellenbergers' home. Tomorrow morning I had to leave for California. Carey told me that he would come to the house to say goodbye early the next day.

It was with rather subdued spirits that Carey and I sat on the sofa the next morning in Charles and Dorothy's front room. We told each other that we were glad we had met and would pray for each other. We exchanged addresses and he handed me a book he had written, just published, and a sealed envelope containing a letter that I decided to read on the plane. Soon it was time for me to leave. We shook hands and Carey and the blue Malibu departed.

Dorothy and a friend who had come to keep her company on the drive home chatted in the front of the car as she drove me to the Austin airport. I appreciated their understanding that I wanted to be quiet. The events of the past three weeks had left me with a great deal to think about. And already I was missing Carey.

As soon as the flight was underway I took out Carey's letter. He wrote that he had wanted to explain more about God's dealings with him in the failure and grief of his divorce. I read eagerly, for last night I had wanted to know more about that, but had not liked to ask.

"In the Bible church in New Jersey of which I was a part," he wrote, "beginning in 1983 our pastor delivered a series of messages directed toward the Christian's inner life and he spoke at length about Psalm 51. This psalm is a very personal prayer of David and I was already quite familiar with it. But as a result of the teaching I took a particular interest in the psalm and found that much of it fit me as though I had written it out of my own experience. I memorized the first thirteen verses. You might read that psalm and think that I may have indulged a groveling, self-loathing spirit—repeating that prayer with a brow-beating, negative attitude. But I can say that I had, by this time, gotten through what a friend called the 'sorrys.' I had repented of my failure in the marriage and really don't think I was heaping abnormal guilt upon myself.

"I learned to recite the thirteen verses, partly as a discipline, and partly because they so expressed my own intent. I wanted God to 'be gracious to me . . . according to His lovingkindness.' I wanted God to 'wash me thoroughly from my iniquity.' I took comfort that God would 'make me to know wisdom' in the 'hidden part' of my life. This was a particularly sad period for me. I had lost my marriage. A nephew had just died of cancer at age 39, I was barely making ends meet, living in a rented room, writing after hours to fulfill a book contract, and working on weekends as a night watchman. And I, who have always enjoyed such health, was having trouble with double vision. Later, this seemed due to stress. The car I was driving was a tired old Buick with retreads, the best I could do. And so I really identified with verse eight: 'Make me to hear joy and gladness, let the bones which Thou has broken rejoice.'

"One form of release I found those days was in running. I could go out and run and pray that psalm phrase by phrase, and in no time I would cover two or three miles. It was a lovely time of prayer and communion for me.

"As I saw that there was no way open for a reconciliation, verse 12 particularly became my prayer. It reads: '. . . Grant me a willing spirit, to sustain me.' During '83 I had come to realize that we may as well be divorced. So, I took the step to file for a divorce.

"The legal process moved very slowly, and that was a good thing, for the Lord was dealing with me. Finally, I came to see that it was not my place to seek a divorce, for I had never wanted our family to break up. I knew that, whatever happened, I wanted a clear conscience and that the children not be hurt further. So, in December 1983, I notified my lawyer and my wife that I was withdrawing my suit for divorce.

"This was a serious step; I knew that to do so could mean that I would go through the rest of my life sort of in limbo, married but not really married. I saw that I should lay down the right to remarriage. David's prayer was mine: 'Grant me a willing spirit, to sustain me.'

"My wife went ahead now and asked for the divorce, which became final in May 1984. That prayer of mine became even more intense, for I sensed a gulf between me and the children.

"So much was happening in my life that I was unwilling for, but there was nothing for me to do but seek God and ask Him to sustain me with a willing spirit. He did, when I was broken and without any strength left. As I found peace through this submitting of my will, I took hope from the next verse: 'Then will I teach transgressors thy ways, and sinners will be converted to thee.' I looked forward, in God's mercy, to that being made true for me and in me.

"I want to thank you, Pam," Carey said, finishing his letter, "for the compassion with which you listened to me last night as we were driving home from Dallas. When I looked at you at the end of my story I saw tears in your eyes."

My mind went back to Mother's advice to me before her death two years ago. Having sensed a tendency in me to hide my feelings she had warned me never to be hard-hearted when it comes to the needs of others. "People are helped when you share joys with them, but also when you share their sorrows," Mother said. And later I had seen through a comment of my sister's that I had an unmerciful attitude toward those who were divorced, tending to put them in a group in my mind and label them all as wrong. I had resolved then to allow God to help me see from His point of view some of the griefs of those who were divorced. He had then let me share with Arlene, my room-mate in Placentia, some of the pain of her divorce. And now in some way I had taken part in Carey's grief.

As the plane traveled on toward Los Angeles I recalled Arlene's divorce. I remembered that in her case the breakup of her marriage had been against her will. And Carey too had just written . . . I flipped open the letter and read again the words—*So much was happening in my life that I was unwilling for, but there was nothing for me to do but seek God and ask Him to sustain me with a willing spirit.*

When he had asked me in the car last night whether I had a single calling it was surely with a deeper meaning than general interest. Was he not telling me that he hoped to remarry one day? Was he thinking that he and I might marry? For that matter, did Carey have the right to marry again?

I did not know. I only knew that I had never felt this way before. Was this what it felt like to be in love with somebody? To have the feeling of being a complete person for the first time? To have a deep desire for his happiness and well-being? Was I overreacting because somebody was showing me unusual interest now that I was in mid-dle age? But, I reminded myself, this was not the first time I had been shown interest by men; I had had a couple of admirers even since Tante Corrie's death. But never before had I had the feelings I was now experiencing.

I prayed that God would not let me take any wrong steps. If our relationship was meant to lead to marriage then I believed it would develop rapidly. If it was not meant to be, it should end very soon.

After spending the night in Los Angeles and retrieving my car from storage, I arrived back at Arlene and Amy's house in Placentia the following evening. Scarcely had we had time to catch up on each other's news when the telephone rang. Arlene answered, then covered the mouthpiece and said, "There is a man wanting to talk to you." She looked very curious.

Carey wanted to know that I had arrived safely and to tell me he would be praying for my speaking appointments in Southern California. Thanking him and telling him I would be in touch, I replaced the receiver. I was aware of feeling deeply happy that he had called. My roommate looked wide-eyed.

"Oh, Arlene," I said, "I have so much to tell you."

She and I talked until late in the evening. I explained all that had happened, concluding with the dilemma I was in. During the coming days I sought God's will earnestly concerning my friendship with Carey. I thought of his repentance, of his having done all in his power to restore his marriage relationship, of his prayers and mobilizing others to pray, and finally of his losing faith that the relationship could ever be restored. And I came to believe that God in His mercy had forgiven him for his own failings and that Carey in free conscience could believe God would give him a new beginning.

And what about my own role? For more than twenty years now I had tried to surrender my will to the Lord. This was surely the most difficult of all these relinquishments—to release to God the possibility that Carey and I might marry. But one night, alone in my little room at Arlene's home, I knelt beside my bed with some reluctance.

"Lord," I began, "You know how hard this is for me." Even as I prayed I knew for the first time for certain that I was in love. How ironic that it was at the moment of releasing Carey that I knew I definitely did not want to. I wanted to *keep* him, not release him. "But, Lord," I said aloud, "You've known this. You've known I'm in love.

Lord, I can only bring You my will, not my feelings. So with my will I surrender Carey to You."

Repeatedly over the next weeks I surrendered Carey to the Lord. Again and again I knelt beside my bed, unsure that I had really been willing to let him go.

Meanwhile, many letters and telephone calls passed between Texas and California. Flowers and perfume arrived from Waco and so, one day, did a small package containing silver earrings with an arrangement of hearts and the note: "If I had this many hearts I would give them all to you."

Carey booked a flight to Los Angeles at Eastertime. Before he came I found that once again, uncomfortably, I was making another prayer of surrender. Many times in the past God had asked me to give up my natural desires. I thought about my first surrender years ago at Ashburnham Place in southern England. I had committed to Him forever my desire to marry. "If You want me to be single in Your service," I had said, "I will be. I will never seek a marriage partner. If You want me to marry, I will trust You to bring somebody to me. I give You all rights to myself."

Alone in Arlene's living room, I resolved before the Lord that I was now not going to go back one inch on what I had promised Him all that time before. How long ago was it? Twenty-one years. Suddenly I was aware of the date. This was March 13, 1986. It was on this exact date, 21 years earlier, that I had been at Ashburnham Place. I was now 42. For the first 21 years of my life I had lived following my own will. For the last 21 years Jesus Christ had been my Lord. Never had I regretted it. My surrender of Carey now must be as real and true a surrender as my original yielding to God all those years before.

Feeling that I knew something of how Abraham felt as

he got ready to sacrifice Isaac, I prepared myself to walk away from Carey.

And then I felt a strong check.

The Lord's sure voice was speaking to me inside my heart: *I have seen the yielding of your love of Carey to Me and I know your submittedness. Now rest. I will guide.*

As simply as that it was over. For twenty-one years I had laid down the issue of marriage. Now, I was no longer being asked to do so. "Thank You, dear Lord."

Almost instantly the nature of my questions began to shift. Would Carey's children accept me? Would financial responsibilities for two families be overwhelming? Would I need to go back to work? Could we afford a home? Would our differing nationalities cause a conflict?

And then I took strength from the fact that although I did not have a blueprint for what lay ahead, the Lord had given me the assurance that He was guiding me in the path that He had chosen for me all along. If God had given Carey to me in His timing, then He would guide us through any rough days that may lie ahead. It would be enough that He knew about them.

Chapter Thirteen

What God Ordained

I looked forward to Carey's visit at Easter. Although I had learned a little about waiting during the years of Tante Corrie's illness, it seemed the end of March would never arrive. Finally, though, on the night before Good Friday at Los Angeles Airport Carey and I were reunited. I moved quickly toward him as he came from the plane, so happy to see his kind face again and, for an instant, teased once more with the question that had come to my mind so often when I first met him: What was it about him that was so familiar?

On Easter Saturday morning, Carey and I headed my car toward the city of Hemet and the home of my father and his wife, Irene. I had told Dad that I wanted to bring a gentleman friend to meet them and we had been invited to lunch. It was wonderful to be with Carey again. Since his arrival two nights before we had taken advantage of every available moment to discuss plans for the future—and we both knew then that our future included marriage. In detail he had spelled out his financial position. We talked about housing in Waco, wondering whether it would be possible for us to buy or rent a small house. We discussed the wedding, deciding that we did not want to

215

wait too long to be married and that California would be the right place for our wedding ceremony.

But there was something missing. Although we both knew it was right for us to marry and talked as if our wedding would soon take place, Carey had not yet said the words "Will you marry me?" As we drove through the palm-lined highways between Placentia and Hemet, I thought about the traditional settings for proposals. A quiet bench in the moonlight with the scent of night jasmine. A candlelit table late one evening in a quiet restaurant. What kind of setting would Carey choose? When was he going to ask me? And would he get down on one knee or two?

On arrival in Hemet we were welcomed into Dad and Irene's cozy home. It had been nearly two years now since their wedding and they had a happy international partnership. Half their year was spent in England and the other half here in Hemet. I could see that Irene had gone to a lot of trouble to prepare a special meal for us. She served ham, potato salad, and vegetables and had even made a casserole of beans prepared according to a Southern recipe she thought would appeal to Carey.

We were about to finish the first course when Carey suddenly addressed a question to Dad.

"Mr. Rosewell," he said, "you have a very nice daughter and I think it is a shame she is not married. I would like to ask you for her hand."

"Well, Carey," said Dad, apparently not one bit taken aback, "that is very nice. But what does she think about it?"

Then Carey turned to me. "Pam," he said, "will you marry me?"

"Yes," I whispered, feeling nonplussed at such a public marriage proposal. This was not how I imagined it would be. But I appreciated deeply that Carey would show respect to my father by officially asking the hand of his middle-aged daughter. This setting was better by far than a bench in the moonlight. And I was aware too of the kindness of the Lord in allowing my father to have a part in the engagement of his eldest daughter whom he must have long assumed would remain single.

Before Carey's plane left for Waco on Sunday night, many plans had been made. We agreed that I would come to Waco in May, and again in August for three weeks, when we hoped to find a place to live. Then, in September 1986, we would be married here in California.

Very quickly, our friendship and love grew. After a somewhat cautious beginning, our friends Charles and Dorothy Shellenberger, when they saw how sure we were of God's leading, gave us their unconditional and very loving support. They told us that when I came to Waco in August they would hold a reception to celebrate our forthcoming marriage.

Carey and I kept in touch daily by phone and through many letters. His easygoing personality had a calming effect on my much more highly strung nature. Many were the times when at the end of telephone conversations Carey gave me a blessing in the name of the Lord. I had never known anybody to do that for me in this way before. It had an extraordinarily calming effect on me as we waited for September.

We tried to make count every minute of the time we were able to spend together. In California we walked on the palm-fringed beaches of the Pacific Ocean and watched the sunset. We hiked trails in the pine-scented San Bernardino Mountains. At springtime in Waco we walked through fields of the most beautiful wildflowers I had ever seen, and made our plans in the shade of spreading live oak trees. I was deeply aware of God's mercy. This was the happiest love affair that I could imagine.

Although many of my friends had met their husbands at a much younger age, I had missed nothing and gained everything by waiting. Repeatedly I thanked God for giving me the grace and faith to wait for His timing.

At the beginning of August I arrived again in Waco. Our main task was to find a place to live. The prices of houses were much lower than in California and we found we would be able to afford a down payment on a small house. We prayed that we would be led to a home with three bedrooms; one for us, one for an office, one for any of Carey's children. Jim, Carey's son, foresaw our need to be alone for a while during our first year together and volunteered to share an apartment with a friend.

On the first evening of our search, Carey and I accompanied a real estate agent on visits to seven houses. The weather was muggy but it was with eagerness that I went with Carey and the real estate man to each front door. Never had I had the opportunity of looking for my very own home. In past years I had been made welcome in many hundreds of homes and had lived in different places on three continents, but never had I had a wall into which I could drive a nail without permission or one I could paint without the approval of its owner.

We were just about to tell the real estate agent that we had done enough viewing for the day when he suggested that we see just one more house. He drove us to an area of town with many trees and even some open spaces, pulling up in front of a small house with a front yard dominated by a large magnolia tree. The lady owner invited us in.

I had not been long inside the little house when it began to feel like home. There were three bedrooms, just as we had wanted. I could imagine the little one overlooking the backyard as our office. I could already see the bookshelves and the joy I would have in unpacking the books and some of Tante Corrie's furniture that had been in storage for so long. On that wall we would place a desk. And the typing table would go there, near the window. Perhaps the day would come when we could even write from our little office. There was a sitting room, dining room, and kitchen and, still a novelty to my European eyes, a laundry room.

But the thing that delighted Carey and me most of all was the roomy back porch, screened in and painted white, with white wicker furniture. It gave a view on the large tree-filled backyard, and the owner, who was moving to smaller accommodations, offered to sell us the wicker furniture very reasonably.

Later that evening we made our decision to buy the little house. We could even assume the mortgage, which meant an additional saving so that Carey could take possession at the beginning of September.

All was now settled and it was time to head for California again, but just before I left Waco, Charles and Dorothy were our hosts at an elegant reception held in one of the town's restored historic homes. Several members of Carey's Texas family were present and so were many old and new friends. It was my official welcome to the community.

On September 13, 1986, Carey and I were married at Rose Drive Friends Church in Yorba Linda, California. My sister, Sylvia, attended me as matron of honor and Digger had flown in too. I was especially glad that Carey's children felt they could participate. His older son, Jon, was best man. His son Jim helped as an usher and Stephanie, his older daughter, took care of the guest book. The church was filled with friends from California and other states much further afield. Charles and Dorothy sat near the front, as did several of Carey's relatives from Texas.

I had chosen a short dress in white Italian prelude satin worn under a long jacket with bead-embroidered lapels and fitted cuffs. I wore a wide-brimmed hat and satin shoes. Sylvia, my only attendant, wore a blue chiffon gown.

It was with a nervousness that surprised me that I accompanied Dad to the front of the church to be presented to my future husband, and I was glad for the firmness with which Carey grasped my hand and arm to help me up the steps to where the minister was waiting for us.

It had been our prayer that the Lord Jesus would be central in our wedding service. We particularly wanted to have a symbol of His love and mercy. We were deeply aware that it was only by His grace that we had been brought together. It was in our Lord's forgiveness that this new beginning was being offered to the two of us.

Deciding that the Communion service would be the best way of remembering the Lord's mercy to us, we asked for it to be part of our wedding ceremony performed by Pastor C. W. Perry. After we had taken our vows we knelt and were served communion by a good California friend, Dr. Ron Rietveld. Together we recited the words of the General Confession from the Book of Common Prayer: "We do not presume to come to this thy table, O merciful Lord, trusting in our own righteousness, but in thy manifold and great mercies. We are not worthy so much as to gather up the crumbs under thy table. But thou art the same Lord, whose property is always to have mercy. . . ."

Our honeymoon was the 1,500-mile journey between Placentia, California, and Waco, and in the last week of September we entered our little home. We decided that during our first year together we would give as much time to each other as possible. And we did. With ever-increasing discoveries of how much we had in common, we sought to establish our new life. The next spring we were glad to welcome Jim to live with us. Still saving for college, he took up residence in the little spare room in the front of the house.

Our first year also held many journeys. I accepted invitations for several speaking engagements and three of Carey's appointments took him out-of-state. I particularly looked forward to his taking part at the yearly writers' conference at Mount Hermon near San Jose in California. I had seen from the prospectus that Tibby Sherrill, whom I had not seen since the time I had worked on the writing of my book nearly three years before, was to be one of the main speakers.

Carey and I arrived at Mount Hermon situated amongst the California redwoods late one evening after the conference had started. After depositing our suitcases in our cabin we made straight for the auditorium where an evening session was in progress. As we walked toward the front of the building, I saw that there were two spare places in a bench on the left. And as we took our seats I saw Tibby in the row behind. We smiled a greeting to each other but there was no opportunity to talk.

When the meeting ended I took the opportunity of introducing Tibby to my husband. After they had talked for a couple of minutes, Carey's attention was claimed by one of the faculty. Tibby took me aside and said: "Pam, do you remember how in Virginia I asked you what qualities you would like in a husband should you ever marry? You asked us to pray for a man who had a deep Christian commitment, who had an interest in writing, and who was gentle and compassionate. You even said you would like to have a good-looking husband. John and I took your request very seriously and we have prayed along those lines often. And," Tibby said, her eyes filled with delight, "when I look at Carey I see the walking answer to our prayers."

I looked at Tibby in amazement. This was the answer to the question that had teased me ever since I had met Carey. Why is he so familiar? I had often asked myself. Now I knew. He was the man who met my description of an ideal husband.

On the first anniversary of our wedding, Carey and I arrived in Mottram in northern England to spend a week with Sylvia and her family. We had come from a visit with family in the south of the country. I had introduced him to Hastings, East Sussex, the town in which I grew up. He had seen the little red brick house in Alexandra Park where the five of us had lived, the old Norman castle, and the English Channel. Now I was looking forward to seeing how he adapted to the very different culture of the north of England.

One day while Carey was exploring the neighborhood, Sylvia and I had a talk. We were once again in her kitchen, the scene of many of our previous conversations. The two older children were in their rooms busy with homework and the twins, who had recently had their tenth birthday, were playing at a schoolmate's house. We knew that we could have a few minutes' uninterrupted conversation.

"What are your plans for this coming year, Pam?" asked Sylvia, rolling out the pastry for one of her apple pies in preparation for supper.

"Well, I would like your advice," I said. "Some of the people who read my book about Tante Corrie have asked if I will write another one."

"And what do you think about that?" asked my sister. I watched as she placed the top piecrust over the prepared apples and began to flute the edges.

"I ask what they suggest I write about," I replied, "and they usually say I should tell of the adventures in a Christian's life when we learn to surrender our wills to His will, and then let Him lead us."

"Do you think you can do that?" Sylvia asked.

"Well, if I did I must be careful not to dwell too much on this very happy marriage," I said. "People would not believe it if I wrote that Carey and I have never had an argument."

Sylvia wiped her hands on her apron and prepared to place the pie in the oven. Very simply she said, "Pam, I believe there is no man in the world more suitable for you than Carey."

And then I looked over Sylvia's shoulder through the window to the moors, still dark and brooding in spite of the September sun. I started to dream. In my mind I could hear the strains of a hymn that had come to me often through the years as I watched the unfolding of God's plan for me.

Hast thou not seen how thy desires e'er have been
granted in what he ordaineth?

"I wonder if I could ever write a story," I said to my sister, "that would describe how afraid I was to give up my desires. How I never wanted to leave England. How I never wanted to speak in public. How I was not prepared to be single in the Lord's service. Yet God has fulfilled my life through the very things I feared. I would so much like to tell people that they have nothing to lose in trusting God with all their lives."

"How would you start the book?" said Sylvia. I could see lots of interest in her steady gray eyes.

"Well," I said, warming to the project, "how about if I start with that day in 1965 in the kitchen of our little house in Alexandra Park when I was so annoyed that you had persuaded me to go to the young people's weekend? That was the start of my big adventure."

"And how would you end it?" asked my sister.

"I do not know," I replied. "Only the Lord sees the end of my story. It is not in my control. But I do know this: when I surrender to Him, I am safer than if I had chosen a known way."